Hiring Contractors Without Going Through Hell

Hiring Contractors Without Going Through Hell

How to Find, Hire, Supervise, and Pay Professional Help for Home Renovations and Repairs

Ellis Levinson

Walker and Company
New York

First published in the United States of America in 1992
by Walker Publishing Company, Inc.

Published simultaneously in Canada by Thomas Allen & Son
Canada, Limited, Markham, Ontario

Library of Congress Cataloging-in-Publication Data
Levinson, Ellis.
Hiring contractors without going through hell : how to find, hire, supervise, and pay professional help for home renovations and repairs / Ellis Levinson.
p.   cm.
Includes bibliographical references (p. tk) and index.
ISBN 0-8027-1194-4 (C).—ISBN 0-8027-7381-8 (P)
1. Dwellings—Remodeling.   2. Dwellings—Maintenance and repair.
3. Contractors.   I. Title.
TH4816.L47   1992
692'.8—dc20   92-7220
CIP

Text design by Brandon Kruse

Printed in the United States of America

2   4   6   8   10   9   7   5   3   1

To Cheryl Smith-Levinson, whose support, encouragement, advice, and love have prodded me into realizing my hopes in a most incredible year. I hope that I shall have the capacity to return these in kind.

Contents

Acknowledgments

I thank the National Association of Homebuilders and the National Association of the Remodeling Industry for their assistance and for their permission to use their exclusive informational materials in this book. HALT, the not-for-profit legal reform organization, was most generous in allowing me to use its contract materials. The American Building Contractors Association of El Monte, California, most generously permitted me to duplicate its Property Improvement Agreement, which appears in Appendix B. And most of all I thank Roger and Barbara Perron for their invaluable assistance and advice.

Introduction: Thinking and Planning

A doctor called a plumber to correct the cause of his flooded basement. The plumber fixed the problem in five minutes and presented his customer with a bill for $150. "This is outrageous!" exclaimed the doctor. "It works out to $1,800 an hour. I'm a surgeon and I don't charge that much."

"I know," responded the plumber. "Neither did I when I was a surgeon."

Death of a loved one
Divorce
Unexpected loss of a job
Moving a considerable distance

What do these events have to do with the subject of this book? They are the only events in life that are usually more traumatic than having major improvements done on your home.

Those who have never gone through the process of adding a bathroom, updating an old-fashioned kitchen, building a second story, or adding another bedroom have no idea how such projects can uproot your life-style and make life's taken-for-granted conveniences suddenly appreciated. The disruption of your boring, banal, babbling existence can lead to such symptoms as desiring the death of the contractor, fantasizing about torturing the workers and subcontractors, hating your own children, and having an unwavering conviction that you need to divorce your spouse, commit arson upon your domicile, collect the insurance money, and abscond to Bangladesh where—surely—life must be better than this hell you're going through.

My wife, who is a psychotherapist, has concluded that victims of major renovations actually go through a grief process. They mourn the loss of their everyday existence: the order, familiarity, predictability, and control they had over their physical abodes.

But there is another aspect of home improvement that compares to major renovations as a mosquito compares to a bumblebee. I am referring, of course, to small to moderate-size home repairs—things like fixing a leaking pipe in your wall, replacing old windows, having your home painted, or installing new vinyl flooring. Sounds easy enough, doesn't it? Heh, heh.

Such small jobs can be unbearably frustrating simply because they carry such an expectation of the ease and speed with which the problem can be corrected. "It's too much for me to take on, so I'll just call Joe the Pro and he'll have it straightened out in just a couple of hours," goes the reasoning. But what if Joe takes *days*? And what if he straightens out the mess in due time okay, but later that evening the problem comes back . . . and he wants to charge you again for him to return and rectify the problem?

If you are a veteran of home renovation or repair nightmares, you know that I do not exaggerate. You know the inconvenience that even a competent effort can bring, to say nothing of the downright havoc that an incompetent or irresponsible contractor can wreak.

Why, you may ask, is the field of home repair such a minefield? Why is it more so than TV repair, auto repair, or furniture refinishing? There are several reasons. An auto mechanic who sets up shop and does poor work is not likely to get repeat customers. He has to invest a fortune in equipment, a shop, licenses, and so on. How long can he stay in business? The same is true of television repair people, although they don't depend as much on repeat customers. But in many areas they must have a business license. Furniture repair people take items out of your home—as do the others—and return them to you. Now any of these can screw up and ruin the job. But they don't work in your home. They don't traumatize your life—with the possible exception of the auto mechanic. They don't disrupt your day-to-day routine, and they don't destroy your home and your everyday conveniences. And lousy contractors can often survive because they don't necessarily depend upon repeat customers. It is true that many contractors depend on word-of-mouth recommendations, and so a lack of such recommendations can hurt their business. But enough advertising in local newspapers and the yellow pages can keep them in business.

If a contractor screws up, correcting the blunder can cause disruption in your life all over again—and induce compound frustrations. The plumbing is defective, so the new bathroom tile has to be ripped up. The newly installed dishwasher backs up, and your kitchen floor is ruined. Sound like enough to make you want to do a Lizzie Borden impression?

According to statistics compiled by the Council of Better Business Bureaus (CBBB), in 1990 home improvement and remodelng companies led all consumer inquiries with more than 14 percent of the total number of inquiries of businesses received by local Better Business Bureaus. And more than 12 percent of all *complaints* were about home improvement and remodeling companies, more than *all* nonautomobile service firms combined.

Included in this group are alarm-system dealers, plumbers, electricians, porcelain refinishing companies, landscapers, painters, wallpaperers, chimney sweeps, swimming pool construction and maintenance companies, heating service contractors, masonry and cement contractors, roofers, and others.

It is the aim of this book to take you by the hand through the wonderland of home renovation and repair. There are lions and tigers and bears (oh my!) in the woods out there. But keep in mind that lions and tigers and bears are not always to be feared, not always creatures of awesome ferocity. They are capable of nobility, strength, and the dogged determination necessary for them to reach their goals.

The trick, on this safari, is to find those creatures that can help and inspire us, that can give us a sense of satisfaction and accomplishment and, yes, even a feeling of added self-worth. And when we happen upon those that need to be tamed in order to achieve our own well-intentioned purposes, we will use techniques that will enable us to get our way— providing we do not expect to achieve the unethical or the impossible.

I suggest that you approach the book in the following way: Read all the chapters even if they don't all seem to apply to your present situation. If you skip chapters you will probably miss important elements in the process of choosing a contractor, getting the work done, and protecting yourself. *Start* each chapter by reading the summary at the *end*. These are easy to locate by looking for the Chapter Summary symbol (a pointing finger). This will give you an overview of the chapter. When you review the summary later, you can check to see if you've retained the information.

Do not hesitate to take notes; doing so can be useful. When I hire a specialty contractor or general contractor, for example, I sometimes review my own notes to make sure that I am following all the right steps. It is difficult to keep all the information in the front of your mind. If you start skipping steps, you create loopholes through which your money and peace of mind may vanish. Don't take short cuts unless you are a gambler.

It seems that there are plenty of books and articles dealing with various aspects of what to ask for from salespeople. But they all omit one thing: to tell you what to do if you are shy, embarrassed, possessed of low self-esteem, easily intimidated, the victim of overbearing parents during childhood, or encumbered by any number of traits that inhibit one from negotiating successfully.

It is easy for an author to say that you should ask for references and then call the references and ask if you can visit their homes and look at the work. We have no trouble telling you to tell the contractor that his work is unacceptable, that you want lien releases, that his prices are too high, that he will have to be more punctual or clean up the mess, or that you're not going to pay until he shows you receipts. And if contractors laugh in your face in an effort to humiliate you or say that they can't accommodate you because company policy won't allow it, what will that do to your ability to do what we authors so glibly instruct?

Recently, my wife witnessed me negotiating with a contractor. He wanted to bolt our house to its foundation (an advisable procedure for folks in quake-prone California who own older homes) without "pulling" a building permit from the city inspection department. We agreed on a price, and then I said to him, "Listen, Ned, this is more than we planned to spend. But I still want to get a permit, and I want it for no extra cost." We spoke for a few minutes, and when he realized that I would give the job to someone else if he didn't give in, he capitulated. Then I made him explain to me in detail all of the processes that would be involved in the work. I made him draw sketches, and when I didn't fully understand them, I asked him to do them again until I knew exactly what he was talking about. I could tell that he respected my diligence. And when he left with a signed contract, we were all happy.

My wife then said to me, "I watched the way you dealt with Ned. You were more assertive than I could ever be. You have the courage to demand what you want. What if the readers of your book don't have that kind of nerve? I think you should deal with it in the book." She was right. (She ain't a shrink for nothing.)

I offer you The Rule of the Psychological Hump. I have devised it for those who are afraid to ask for what they are entitled to. Any time during the process that you feel afraid of asserting yourself, I want you to take a deep breath and say, "This is my home. This is my money. I am entitled to get what I want because I am dealing in a fair and ethical manner for something I deserve." Then steel your nerves and ask for— no, demand—what you want. The worst thing that can happen is that you will be rejected. But don't necessarily settle for that either. Rejection and intimidation are disheartening only to those who *will* take no for an answer. Get over that psychological hump.

Hiring Contractors Without Going Through Hell

1

Finding a Contractor

"I'll be right over," said the plumber. When he arrived six hours later, he asked, "How is everything?"

"Not bad," responded the homeowner. "My wife always wanted to learn how to swim."

BEFORE I DISCUSS HOW TO HIRE A CONTRACTOR, LET'S define what we mean by a contractor. Technically, a contractor is anyone who is party to a contract—specifically, one who contracts to perform a service. We are concerned here particularly with those people who contract to do home improvements or repairs as well as those who hire, supervise, and coordinate craftspeople and suppliers to perform home improvements. Those in the latter group are referred to as *general contractors*. In other words, for our purposes, a general contractor is a professional builder or remodeler who takes charge of a construction job and coordinates the work of the craftspeople and their helpers, suppliers, the designer or architect (if one is involved), local building inspectors and related government agencies, and any other factions or factors that might come into play. General contractors themselves may or may not perform some or all of the work, depending upon the type and size of the job and upon the nature of the operation that they run.

Some general contractors are one-person operations in which the contractor handles all, or most, of the work herself with the help of an assistant or two. These contractors need to be personally proficient in plumbing, carpentry, hanging drywall, electrical wiring, and any number of other skills. Few can do it all competently.

Finding the Candidates

Keep in mind that finding a reliable contractor will ultimately lead to a feeling of satisfaction—if not relief—once the job is done, or the problem is fixed, in a timely and competent manner. Using an uncaring, incompetent, or unprofessional professional can lead to anger, frustration, depression, and even a blow to your self-esteem. So do your self-esteem and your feelings of competence and accomplishment a favor: Knuckle down and go through the short-term effort of finding yourself a good contractor.

The question becomes: How do I find a reliable contractor? I kid you not when I say that this is one step short of asking: Where would I find the Holy Grail? It seems to be the great mystery of home-owning America. First, let me give you places *not* to look:

> *The yellow pages.* Anyone who can afford to pay for a slick display ad can make him- or herself look very good in the phone book.
> *Mail advertising.* Same reasons.
> *A handwritten ad on the bulletin board of a local building-supply store or supermarket.* It could be a guy who last week was taking a course on how to pass the general contractor's license exam . . . and he may not have passed.
> *Door-to-door solicitations.* I have never heard of a door-to-door solicitation that turned out to be a legit job, done in a competent manner, by a licensed professional who could write a literate sentence. I suppose that such instances have occurred, but so did (many believe) the stopping of the sun in the sky for the battle of Jericho. There are so many scams by which gullible homeowners are victimized by shrewd operators that you have to be desperate beyond comprehension, under the influence of hallucinogenic drugs, or trusting beyond reason to go along with street solicitors.

"Okay, Wisenheimer," I hear you asking, "how *do* I find a reliable, legitimate contractor?" Start by asking yourself this question: "Whom do I know who has had work done on his or her property and has been satisfied with the outcome of that experience?" That acquaintance may know the right person to do the job for you. Keep in mind that we are talking about work that is similar to the job that you need done. The fact that your cousin had a new deck built in her back yard and just loves it does not mean that the carpenter who built it will be sufficiently competent to install cupboards and cabinets in your kitchen. The exactitude required for finished cabinetry is not the same as that which is required for the outdoor installation of rough-hewn lumber. But it may be a starting point. If the craftsperson was reliable, clean, reasonably priced, and punctual, it may be worth your time to at least discuss the project with her and ask her about her skills.

Remember, if you are looking for a plumber to install a new bath and shower, you are not looking for any old reliable plumber. You are looking for someone who is experienced at installing large fixtures—a person who has dealt with complications with flooring, drywall, tile, and any number of combinations of circumstances that could be associated with the installation.

Now, let's say that you find someone who loved her contractor (well, not literally—such involvement could fog her judgment). You will want to look at the job. What might appear to be beautiful work to someone else could be second-rate in your eyes. Have you ever met a person who just loved his plastic surgeon, but you're wondering why anyone would want his nose to look like a spoon with two holes in the end?

Suppose that you are a despicable human being who has been disowned by your family and who has no friends. Where do you go for a referral? If you have ever had satisfactory dealings with a contractor in a field other than the one in which you need work done, that might be a start. Suppose, for example, that you have used an electrician with whom you were satisfied, and you need plastering work done. Electricians often work with plasterers to patch up the holes that the electricians make when doing repairs or installations. If you feel that he or she is trustworthy, you could ask the electrician to refer a dependable plasterer. Plasterers often know drywall contractors, painters, and carpenters. And so on.

Suppliers are often good sources for reliable contractors—if you're careful. If you are looking for a plumber, a plumbing-supply house is an obvious place to start. Telephone companies in many parts of the country provide *Business to Business Yellow Pages* to their customers upon request. You can find "Plumbing Fixtures, Parts & Supplies—Wholesale" listed there. If no such *Business to Business* book is available in your area, look for plumbing suppliers in your regular yellow pages. You can visit such a business and ask the manager or proprietor to direct you to a reliable plumber. Tell the manager that you are looking for someone who can handle the type of job you need done. If she gives you the name of a candidate, ask the following questions:

- Have you—or do you know anyone who has—used this person's services? Were you/they satisfied?
- Is this a pleasant and earnest person?
- Does he always pay his materials bills on time? Have his checks ever bounced?
- Does the person use competent helpers or does he simply pick up day workers when needed?
- Have you ever recommended this person before? If so, what were the results?

In a like manner, you can find a tile contractor at a tile dealer, a flooring repair person at a flooring supplier, a carpenter through a lumberyard, and so on.

Another source—though hard to locate—is professional and trade associations. An organization that represents the interests of, let's say, carpenters may be able to refer you to a professional who specializes in meeting your particular needs.

Locating one of these professional associations, however, can be as easy as threading a needle while riding in a New York City taxicab. The first place to look is in the yellow pages under the heading "Associations." The Greater Los Angeles Pacific Bell Yellow Pages lists such organizations as "National Electrical Contractors Association," "Carpenters Local Union No. 309 A. F. of L.," and "Plumbing and Piping Industry Council, Inc." The listings are not always alphabetically arranged by specialty under the headings. You may, therefore, have to peruse the listings to find the organization you are looking for in a nonalphabetized position. Note that not all such associations are set up to make referrals; some are simply unions, lobby groups, or public relations organizations.

If you are unable to locate a helpful referral agency under a yellow pages listing, you might want to try the following approach. Look under the listings for the type of contractor you need. For instance, if you need a plumber to install a new toilet, look under "Plumbing Contractors." But also look for display ads from contractors who deal with specialized plumbing services that *do not* deal with what you need—perhaps a drain rooter service. Remember, you do not want to take a random shot at picking an unrecommended contractor.

Call and ask which professional association plumbers might belong to. (This information might even appear in some of the yellow pages display ads of various plumbers.) Then locate the association and ask for a referral to a professional who can meet your particular needs. Such associations have a vested interest in referring you to someone who is reputable. First of all, if the carpenter to whom you are referred turns out to be a blockhead, it is likely that you are going to try to nail the referring organization. Second, if the plumber to whom you were referred turns out to be a pipehead, it implies that all plumbers are trying to drain off your money.

Referral services exist in some more populous areas. Finding them, however, can be difficult. They are often hard to find because you don't know where to look. The one I am aware of in Los Angeles publicizes itself through mail advertising. You might try looking under "Contractors," "Contractors—Alteration," "Contractors—Remodeling," or a similar designation in the yellow pages and scanning the columns for a referral service. Or ask friends if they know of a referral service. This is the hardest source to locate. Such services gather a stable of contractors in all fields of home and real estate improvement and repair. In theory, they check out the craftspeople's credentials and references. They recommend such professionals based on the customer's needs, price range, and location. You must be careful, however. Do not rely simply on the recommendations of the referral services. Remember, they make their money by collecting fees from the people they recommend. Once the craftsperson is paid by the homeowner, he or she pays a fee or commission to the referral service.

Ask the referral agency for at least three referrals so that you can compare several candidates. If it is reputable, the agency will want to offer you a selection of candidates because it wants you to find a person who fits your needs and personality so that you are less likely to look elsewhere for someone to satisfy your needs. Sounds like a singles bar.

Before calling a candidate who is referred to you by a referral agency, ask the agency a few questions:

- Are all of your craftspeople licensed (or registered, if your state requires or offers such licensing)?
- Do you require your service professionals to be bonded

or insured? If you don't, will you tell me which ones aren't?

- In case of a dispute, do you help to resolve the conflict?
- What is your policy in terms of customer complaints?
- Will you tell me of any customer complaints against any of the service people you refer?

Keep in mind that if any of these criteria are not met, you will have to decide for yourself whether or not you want to proceed with the referral service. It could be that many of the referrals will meet your criteria, such as carrying a bond, even if not required to do so by the service. And even if the referring agency does restrict its clients to those who meet all of the licensing, bonding, and insurance criteria, you will have to double-check the candidates yourself. More about this in Chapter 2.

The observant consumer might come upon another source. Have you ever passed by a house that was undergoing remodeling or was having an addition put on and thought to yourself, "I hope I have sex tonight"? Well, if so, good luck. But if you wondered whether the work crew was any good, whether the contractor was competent, or whether the home-owners were satisfied with the progress of the work, then you should know that you have access to some vital information. You can go to the owner of that property and ask her whether she is satisfied with her contractor. Is he easy to work with? Clean? Punctual? Does he adapt to changes well? Does the contractor live up to the terms of the contract? When the job is finished, ask the owners about their final impressions of the work—especially the quality of the work with particular attention to details. If the overall response is excellent, you have a good reference.

Architects

Let's briefly discuss architects as a source of referrals. As you will find out in Chapter 7, architects are not always good references for contractors. If the contractor and the architect have a kickback arrangement or if they collude on projects in order to mutually maximize their profits, you could get—as we used to say in the Bronx—a royal screwing. So I can only advise you to double your precautions before deciding upon a contractor who was recommended by an architect.

You will first have to decide whether an architect is needed for the job. Obviously, this issue is relevant only if you are remodeling. You won't need an architect for new flooring, for a new roof, or for changing lighting or plumbing (although you may want to consult a plumbing engineer or a lighting consultant). Larger reputable general contracting firms often have their own designers or architects. You can shop around to determine your needs. However, if you are not using an architect for a particular job, you may want to ask one for a referral to a contractor upon whom he or she feels you may rely. Perhaps you know such an architect, or a friend can refer you to one he trusts.

You may want to consult with a local government building official to determine whether a design engineer or architect might be needed for the project you have in mind.

How do you find architects? You can consult with the American Institute of Architects (AIA), a professional trade organization that has chapters in virtually every municipality. The AIA can recommend candidates who specialize in the type of project you have in mind.

You may also use the same sources you would use in finding contractors. Personal referrals are always a prime source. You should run the same checks on an architect that you would run on a contractor (see Chapter 2).

You will of course need to find out the candidates' experience with the type of project you have in mind and what services they will provide—including oversight of the job, fees, additional costs, references, and so on. If you follow the guidelines for contractors in Chapter 2, you should do all right.

The AIA provides standard forms for agreements between architects and owners, between architects and contractors, and among all three parties.

If you are remodeling on a large scale, it will probably pay for you to hire an architect—unless you find a contractor who has a staff that is proficient in design. We are now stuck with the chicken-or-the-egg question. If you are pondering which to pick first, shop around for both and see what you find. If you decide on one of each, have them get together in your presence and see how well they consult with each other. My contractor friend is reluctant to work with architects' plans. He prefers to have his designer come up with original plans that fit the contractor's building approach. If the client insists on using an architect, my friend requires the client to pay a fee to see that the plans are complete and to go over and adapt the plans to fit his own way of working.

For more helpful and detailed information on selecting and dealing with architects, you can write for *Consumer's Guide to Hiring an Architect,* California Board of Architectural Examiners, Box 944258, 1021 O Street, Room A102, Sacramento, CA 94244–2580. It contains excellent information—no matter where you live. If you decide to hire an architect for the job, I strongly advise you to obtain this publication. Yeah . . . it's free.

More About Credentials

I have spent most of my life in New York City. And while I always thought that a large percentage of the city's drivers were nuts, I had an unconscious expectation that they were competent at handling their vehicles. When I first visited Los Angeles—and then Miami—I reasoned that having a driver's license meant different things in those places from what they did in The Big Apple. How, I wondered, could a Californian who had a license not know that you should—nay, must—signal before making a turn? And was it not universally understood—even in Dade County—that when driving on a highway with a fifty-five-miles-per-hour speed limit you do not drive at thirty-five miles per hour in the left lane?

So I talk generally about licensing in the field of contracting, even though it could be a whole different thing in Alabama from the way it is in Alaska. Being a licensed contractor in some states could mean that a person has paid a small fee to register for a license. Period. Thirty-five states now require individuals to register or to obtain a license, although only about twelve of them require testing. California has stringent requirements for all types of home repair and improvement contractors.

If you do not know the requirements for contractors in your locale, get in touch with your local department of consumer affairs, which should be able to tell you what the general requirements are for a professional to call himself a plumber, electrician, general contractor, and so on. Refer to Appendix A for an overview of respective state requirements and regulatory agencies.

And don't assume that someone who has a license is necessarily competent. I was watching "Geraldo" one afternoon and heard one horror story after another as people described the mistakes that surgeons had made on their patients. I decided right then that if I ever needed an operation I would write notes with a Magic Marker on my body so that the surgeon wouldn't cut the wrong thing. I pictured myself with a sign on my leg: "Wrong leg. Please operate on my *left* knee." All this is just my way of saying that if a physician with twelve or more years of demanding post–high school training can make stupid mistakes, imagine what a guy who might have dropped out of the tenth grade could do to your home.

At this point, let's put a few of these elements together. If you feel that the job is likely to be a costly one by your own standards, you will want to get estimates from at least three candidates for the job. This does not mean that you will make just three initial phone calls. One of the contractors you call might be too busy to take on the job. Or the job might be too small. The location might be inconvenient. You may dislike the contractor's tone of voice, his inability to communicate clearly (an absolutely essential requirement), or his unwillingness to accommodate your schedule in order to set up an appointment. Have you ever talked with a stranger on the phone and realized that you dislike this person and aren't even sure why? (If you haven't, you are a more open, kind, and nonjudgmental being than we mortals.) In short, there are lots of reasons why you might not seek estimates from particular contractors. You want to find three actual contenders for the job.

Dealing with the Contractor

When I think of calling a contractor who is a stranger, I remember with mixed emotions when friends would set me up with potential blind dates. I would call the lucky young woman with enthusiasm about the possibility of a new relationship and with apprehension about how I might do in trying to meet her needs and wants—and vice versa. I would also, of course, fear that she would turn out to have any number of horrendous physical or psychological traits. How does this relate to contractors? Guess. Yup. Same thing, except for the sexual tension.

The initial phone call is your first opportunity to start separating the wheat from the chaff. (I'll be honest; I'm not sure what that phrase actually means.) A few select questions will enable you to determine if this is even a reasonable candidate for the job.

If you live in a state or locale that licenses or registers contractors, *ask the candidate whether he or she is licensed or registered.* Forget about candidates who aren't. Reliable contractors cherish their licenses. They make them legitimate. If they are not licensed, there won't be much you can do, short of legal action, to force them to honor their contracts. Contractors *want* to have licenses so that they can show that they are legitimate professionals. There are, of course, highly skilled professionals who do not have licenses. A person can be a damned good plumber without having a license. But why *doesn't* that plumber have a license? Could it be that he once killed an old lady by accidentally hooking her toilet waste pipe up to the kitchen faucet, and now the cops are looking for him? Could it be that he is just too lazy to study for the license exam?

Perhaps his ethics don't float and in case he decides to screw someone royally, he doesn't want a regulatory agency breathing down his neck.

If you need a small plastering job done and your next-door neighbor has used an unlicensed guy a couple of times and she raves about him, go for it. You don't have too much to lose. (Although, quite honestly, I once hired one of these guys from a neighborhood newspaper ad, and he did a lousy job for 150 bucks.) These people are usually cheaper than licensed contractors, but it is more difficult to determine which of them is competent.

Ask whether the contractor is bonded. A bond, in this instance, is an insurance policy for which the contractor pays a premium. It guarantees that the contractor will meet his obligations in a satisfactory manner. Failure to do so should result in the payment of compensation by the bonding company. However, this is a limited surety bond and is not sufficient for large jobs. I will discuss this in more detail in Chapter 2.

Ask whether the contractor carries liability and workmen's compensation insurance. These policies protect you from legal actions in case of injuries to visitors or to contractors' employees, respectively. More about this in Chapter 2.

Ask how long the contractor has been in business doing this type of work. If this is a new company, move on, unless it's a simple job and the contractor can convince you that he has the know-how and experience to do the job right. One estimate I have come across says that 95 percent of all home improvement contractors go out of business within five years. Five years, I believe, is a good minimum for you to look for in a contractor's experience.

If you have a time limitation for the job, *determine whether he or she can plan the job to fit your schedule.*

If a contractor fails to meet any of these criteria, you would probably be wise to look elsewhere for a candidate.

Deciding on Your Needs

If you are calling about a straightforward repair like a leaking roof or broken bath tiles, it is simple for you to explain the problem, tell the contractor that you want an estimate, and set up an appointment—the exception being when you have an emergency. But if you want to replace your bath fixtures, add a room, or remodel your kitchen, you should have an idea in advance of what you want to do.

It's hard to decide on whom you should hire if you don't know what it is you want. Confer with family members and decide whether you can live with the wall tiles in the bathroom even though you will be changing the flooring and fixtures. As long as you're redoing the kitchen, should you pay the extra money to put in a pantry? If you're thinking about a swimming pool, should you consider a Jacuzzi while the pool work is being done?

Consider exactly how the proposed changes will affect the house and the way it runs. Will your family grow or shrink? (This is not a diet question.) Will it affect the house's marketability or value? Can it be undone if your needs change?

Before you start pulling ideas out of the air, it's time to go to a newsstand or library and start looking through magazines like *Good Housekeeping, House Beautiful, Architectural Digest, Woman's Day, Family Circle,* and anything else that might have decorating ideas. Your librarian or newsdealer should be able to assist you.

Start thinking about price. Don't begin negotiations with contractors without having an expectation of what you are willing to pay and how much you can afford or borrow. Otherwise, anything the contractors suggest will sound like a great idea: "We can put in a below-ground swimming pool and bowling alley for just another $1,000."

"That's all? Good idea!"

A rule of thumb for those who are concerned with the value of their homes after remodeling is this: Don't improve the home so that it is worth more than 15 percent more than the highest-value home in the neighborhood. The reason for this is that you will not normally be able to get that money back when you sell your home. Buyers and banks are not fond of sinking money into property that's priced a lot higher than anything else in the area.

If you are thinking of expanding your home, check your title insurance for restrictions on such construction. And check zoning limitations as well with your local zoning administration office. Will the expansion be so large that it will necessitate that all parts of the home conform with the current building code?

Draw a sketch or sketches of the ideas you have in mind. You don't have to be Leonardo da Vinci in order to scratch out an idea of what the contractor and/or architect will be aiming for. These drawings will help you determine whether your needs for a particular room can be met. You might even want to make rudimentary two-dimensional cutouts of furniture, appliances, and the like to see how well they can be accommodated in a floor plan.

Example: I have two friends named Jerry and Arleen. They noticed that the roof on their house was starting to look as if it had just been strafed by an enemy fighter plane. A friend recommended a reliable roofer, so they called him and made an appointment. The roofer, Mr. Shakes, was busy and couldn't come to give the estimate for almost two weeks. He arrived at the scene, looked over the job, and asked what they had in mind.

"My aunt had polyurethane foam put on her roof, and she just raves about it. That's what we'd like," said Arleen.

"I do shingles, tile, hot mop, cold tar, roll composition, and almost anything else," said Mr. Shakes. "But I don't spray foam. I'm sorry. Anyway, I guarantee my composition work for five years."

"Jeepers," said Jerry. "Aunt Dinah got a ten-year guarantee with her roof."

"Sorry, folks. Had I known, I coulda saved time and trouble for you and me both."

What is the lesson here? If Jerry and Arleen knew that they wanted a specific application, they should have asked Mr. Shakes about it on the phone. They would be two weeks ahead of the rain. And while they're at it, they should ask about the guarantee as well. And they forgot one of the cardinal rules. When they were given the recommendation from their friend, they didn't ask if the roofer performed the *same type of work* they wanted done.

Once you are sure that you have a good candidate on the phone and are reasonably sure that he or she is qualified for your specific job, make an appointment. But you don't have to wait until you get an estimate from the first contractor before you set up a meeting with the others. That approach could drag the process out endlessly.

It is not a good idea for you to set up the appointments immediately following one another. Each contractor whom you call for a large-scale job will give you different approaches, options, and design and material suggestions. You will want to mull over the new ideas that hadn't occurred to you before. You can then run them past the other candidates when they come to look at the job. The new suggestions might also stimulate you into some creative thinking.

If the job you are contemplating involves design—such as remodeling, additions, wallpaper or paint, or new flooring—make sure that all family members concerned are present for the contractor's presentation (okay, the baby doesn't have to be there for the new nursery planning) so that one spouse doesn't make choices that will cause the end of the marriage. And so your teenage son doesn't go on a lawn-mowing strike because you picked pink floral wallpaper for his lair.

I don't want you to get the impression that you need three estimates for every job. If you find a tiler to redo your lavatory and you like her and she comes recommended and the price seems reasonable and she conducts herself in a professional way—go for it. Don't drive yourself nuts over a simple job. Besides, if you drag out the process after the first contractor gives you an estimate for a relatively small $900 job, by the time you reject the next two contractors' estimates the original contractor may conclude that you are a pain in the butt and decide that he doesn't need the work that badly.

Things to Remember

1.   A contractor, as far as this book is concerned—is a person who contracts to make repairs upon or improvements to your home or property.

2.   For major repairs or improvements, solicit enough contractors for estimates so that you are left with at least three candidates for the job.

3.   To find candidates for the job, try these sources: a friend or relative who has had *similar* work done; other contractors whose judgment you trust; professional trade associations; suppliers who trade in equipment and supplies for the type of contractor for which you are looking; referral services; owners of local houses that are undergoing renovation, repair, or expansion (if you are looking for a general contractor or carpenter, etc.); and architects (with extra precautions).

4.   When you call candidates for the job, ask if they:
Perform the specific type of work you require
Are licensed in that particular field (if applicable in the area in which you live)
Are bonded
Carry workmen's compensation and liability insurance
Also ask how long they have been in business doing this type of work, and, should you decide to hire them, how soon the work can begin.

5.   Schedule your estimate meeting at a time when all concerned family members can be there.

6.   Allow sufficient time between contractor appointments.

2

Deciding on a Contractor

Joe: Use my plumber.
Moe: Is he dependable?
Joe: Definitely. He's fixed my toilet lots of times.

General Contractors

You have followed the recommendations in Chapter 1 and have three seemingly worthwhile contenders for the job. The question remaining is, "How do I choose between them?"

Let Your Guts Be Your Guide

I will tell you the story of the first major contracting job we ever had done.

The dilapidated old kitchen in the rental unit of our duplex was in dire need of upgrading. Cheryl and I called our local contractor/home repair referral service, which gave us a list of licensed remodelers who could modernize the place. We also called Sears. The Sears estimator informed us that the company's professionals work basically on cabinets, doors, countertops, and the like. They make no structural, plumbing, or electrical modifications. I believe the reason for this is that Sears and other large chains merely subcontract this work out to local contracting firms and take responsibility for the work. It would be too complicated for them to do estimates for endlessly complex jobs involving multiple subcontractors.

The first contractor from the referral service—let's call him Johnny, as in Johnny-come-lately—called to cancel his first appointment and then showed up late for his second appointment. Although he had just put himself out of the running, we decided to have him do the estimate anyway. We reasoned that we should at least get ideas from him and use his estimate as a point of reference.

The second contractor, Roger, was precisely on time. He spoke professionally and made no attempt to hard-sell us. He showed us photographs of his work and letters of recommendation. He asked us about our needs and expectations. Our gut reaction was that we really liked him as a person. He had samples of countertop materials and brochures of various ready-made cabinets. And he came up with some creative suggestions. He told us that it would take some time for him to price the supplies needed and to get estimates from his subcontractors and that he would get back to us with an estimate. When Roger left, Cheryl said that she had a good feeling about him and that he would probably be her choice. I cautioned that we were on a strict budget and that price would have to enter into it.

The third contractor—whom I'll call Oakie—seemed professional enough. He seemed to know what he was doing. But he lacked warmth and humor. He also suggested a way to add a center window to the kitchen wall. He came back with an estimate of about $8,500, which beat Roger's estimate by almost $3,000 and would include the new window.

Although we felt better about Roger, we couldn't resist the financial savings and extra window. And since both of them had good references, we went with Oakie.

Several days before work was to begin, Oakie called us. "I'm sorry. I made a mistake. And if you want to cancel the order, I understand," he began. I could feel my face turning red with anger.

"What's up?" I responded.

"Well, I made a mistake when I calculated your estimate. Somehow I left out the cost of purchasing the kitchen cabinets."

"How could that be?" I asked. "The cabinets are the largest part of the job."

"Yeah, I know. I'm real sorry."

I had to ask. "How much more will it cost?"

"About another $6,000," he responded with shame in his voice.

Needless to say, that ended our business dealings with Oakie. This type of "mistake" is a dead giveaway. Even if it was an honest error, it showed that this contractor was capable of sloppy work and huge miscalculations.

The worst part of the whole thing was that I had to listen to Cheryl say about half a dozen times, "I *knew* we should have gone with Roger." We did hire Roger, and he did a great job for us, just as we anticipated he would.

So what is the lesson here? When trying to decide on a contractor, one of the factors to consider is your guts. Very often that gut feeling is your unconscious mind telling you that something either feels right or is terribly suspect. However, if you are one of those people who are extremely trusting and gullible, you may want the help of the guts of someone you respect and trust before factoring your own feelings into the equation.

But your own negative feelings about the contractor should not be discounted. They come up for a reason. In the case of Roger and Oakie, our gut feelings were right on the money. As it turned out, Roger was the less expensive and more reliable professional. And he did such a good job for us that we felt that the money was well spent.

Here are some reasons why your guts might get that queasy feeling:

- You can't verify the address and phone number of the contractor.
- The salesperson says that your home will be used for advertising as a showplace of the contractor's work and that a sign will be placed out front.
- The contractor avoids giving you references.
- You are asked to pay a large amount in advance (see Chapter 3).
- You are asked to make your deposit check out to the salesperson instead of to the company, or you are asked to pay cash.
- The salesperson uses high-pressure tactics to get you to sign a contract. Typical methods include scare tactics, intimidation, or outright threats. One popular ploy often employed by car salespersons is the "I will only offer you this price right now. If you don't accept this offer I will not be able to make it again." Don't fall for it.

A person who tries to push you into making a deal is hungry and is interested only in your money, not in what benefits you. If you are a tough negotiator, you can use that hunger to your own benefit. You could lead such a salesperson on until she is ready to close in for the kill. And just when she thinks she has you in her clutches—when her expectations are high—you are in a position to pull back and make more demands. This approach may sound ruthless, but I have no sympathy for anyone who tries to negotiate with people by taking advantage of them.

I recommend that you rent the movie *Tin Men* to get an idea of the techniques used by ruthless salespeople. You must be sure, however, before you get into a negotiation with such people, that you are willing to deal with them for the duration of the job.

You should not feel like a racist, a chauvinist, or a xenophobe (excuse me, but I so seldom get to use that word) if you feel uncomfortable dealing with someone because you don't like the way he or she handles the English language. Nothing can screw up a job easier than a nod of the head from someone who doesn't have any idea what you're talking about (refer to Ronald Reagan and the Iran Contra Scandal for further elucidation). If you had a toothache, would you go to a dentist who wasn't fluent in English? And telephone communication gets even worse.

The Psychological Hump

If you have not read the introduction to this book, I am giving you an assignment: *Read it!* In particular, this is the place where The Rule of the Psychological Hump comes in. Starting here, you will be asked to make assertions, demands, requests, counteroffers, and refusals. It is from this point on that you must assert your self-worth, your right to get what is fairly yours, and your power to reject what is not healthy or fair to your well-being. So, if you are not an assertive or strong-willed person, I want to get you into the practice of taking a deep breath and saying to yourself: "This is my home. This is my money. I am entitled to get what I want because I am dealing in a fair and ethical manner for something I deserve." Then steel your nerves and go for it.

References, References, References

No reputable businessperson should hesitate to provide you with references. A professional should take pride in her work and be willing to show you her achievements. This applies whether it's a nose job, a work of art, or a new bathroom. When you have narrowed down your choices to two or three candidates, it is time to check out their references. Keep in mind that there are two types: verbal references and on-site inspections.

When Roger the contractor saw how satisfied we were with his work, he asked me to write a letter of recommendation so that he could add it to the file he shows to prospective customers. Since then, I have received many calls from Roger's prospective customers who wish to confirm the positive comments in my letter.

None of them, however, ask if they may come over and see the work that Roger did. This would be the second type of reference—the one where the contractor arranges for satisfied customers to show a job or two or three to prospective clients. If you are having any type of remodeling or home improvement done, I strongly recommend that you use both types of references. A contractor who has no verifiable letters of recommendation has to be suspect. Surely *someone* out there must have liked his work.

Contractors should also be eager to show you work that either is in progress or was recently completed. If they make excuses, you have reason to be suspicious. And make sure that the work you are looking at is similar to the work you will be contracting for. If you are adding on a new bathroom, it does you little good to see a wood deck that a contractor recently built.

There is a psychological aspect to all of this. Many people fear calling up a stranger and saying, "Listen, you don't know me, but what do you think of Oakie the contractor? Is he a nice guy? Did he do good work?" If you are one of those people, rest assured that you have nothing to fear. Remember that the contractor has already received permission from these past customers to use them as references and to have people call. It is my experience that customers are so thrilled to have found a good contractor that they are delighted to share their discovery with the world.

Asking if you may come over and look at the completed job is a somewhat more gutsy move. Many people do not want strangers traipsing through their kitchens or other parts of their homes. So when you ask the contractor for references, make sure that she provides you with the names of former clients who will be willing to show you the actual improvements.

Keep in mind that there are some categories of work the results of which it is difficult, if not impossible, to examine. These include plumbing, central air-conditioning, in-wall insulation, electrical wiring, and termite control.

If you actually examine three work sites for three different contractors, you will be making nine trips and who-knows-how-many phone calls. I advise that you start with one customer visit per contractor and that you do your inspections, one per contractor, in three rounds. This way, if you find a bad job, or one which shows that the work is not of the type that meets your expectations, you can eliminate that contractor without further inspections.

The Questions

There are two types of questions you must ask: those directed at the contractor and those directed at the contractor's previous customers.

You'll want to ask the contractor some basic questions. However, the questions you will need answered will vary with your needs. The more complex the job, the more subcontractors will be involved. Just let the questions flow and write down the answers. You will never be able to remember which contractor gave which answer if you don't write it all down.

Here are the basic questions you will want to ask the contractor:

1.   How much will various options cost?
2.   How long will the job and its various components take?
3.   What is your previous experience? Do you have photos of previous jobs?
4.   Do you have a particular interest in this project? Do you have any special skills that you bring to this particular type of job?
5.   Do you belong to any professional organizations? (The National Association of Home Builders Remodelors Council [NRC] and the National Association of the Remodeling Industry [NARI] are two of the more prominent ones.) If the answer is yes, ask whether the contractor abides by the association's arbitration procedures. If she says that she does, ascertain from the organization that her answer is truthful.
6.   What type of warranty do you offer on your workmanship and materials?
7.   Are you licensed (in those states or locales that license)?
8.   Are you bonded? Do you offer a completion bond?
9.   Are you insured for workmen's compensation and liability?

10. Do you have your own crew? How much of the work is subcontracted out? Do you hire day laborers?
11. Who are your subs (subcontractors) and suppliers?

The last two types of questions should be asked at the end of your initial interview if you are still interested in the contractor. Most general contractors either sub out all of their work or do a major part of it with their own crew and sub out only specialized work.

The Subs

I strongly recommend that you be especially careful about people who use day laborers, who often are people who stand around on certain street corners or in building-supply dealers' parking lots, hoping to be selected by a contractor who may drive up and offer work for a day or two to people whom he does not know and may never see again. In certain parts of the country they are non–English speaking and are sometimes illegal aliens. I personally would not want to have a staircase built by someone who has limited understanding of a supervisor's language and who is being exploited for low wages.

Most general contractors—especially in locales that regulate them—have some knowledge of or expertise in most areas of home improvement. However, very few of them are qualified to *perform* repairs or improvements in every possible area. Therefore, in a major home improvement job, it makes sense that a considerable part of the work will be subcontracted out to those professionals who specialize in areas where the contractor's crew might be deficient. So if one contractor claims that he won't be using subs because his outfit is qualified to do it all, be careful.

Example: Jerry and Arleen decided to add a second floor that would have a bedroom and bathroom. One of the candidates to do the job was Barry's Better Builders.

"Who are some of your subcontractors?" asked Arleen.

"We don't use subs. We do it all ourselves," responded Barry proudly.

"You have a bathroom tile guy on your crew?" asked Jerry.

"Billy."

"Electrician and lighting guy?" asked Arleen.

"Bubba."

"Plumber?"

"Bobby."

"Plasterer?"

"Benjie."

Arleen mentioned a carpenter to frame the additions and build a staircase.

"Bobby."

"Bobby does that as well as the plumbing?"

"Yep. And he also does the drywall and plastering."

"Paint and wallpaper?"

"Bubba."

"Your electrician hangs wallpaper?"

You get the idea. The question remains: So what are the disadvantages of using a contractor who doesn't subcontract any of the work? There are at least three. First, as in the case just cited, such general contractors may be overstretching their talent and that of their crews. This is why it is important to check out the jobs they have done for other clients.

Second, subcontractors are a good source of references in regard to general contractors' reputations. More about this coming up.

Third, during the course of the project, some subcontractors can be asked in confidence how they think the overall job is going. This can be a great aid in checking up on contractors as the work progresses.

Why do you want to know who the subcontractors are? They can be a great aid in determining how reliable a prospective contractor is in paying her bills. After you are told which parts of the job are to be subbed out, ask the contractor for the names of the subs. Call some of the suppliers and ask about the general contractor. "Do you know her to be a satisfactory (or terrific, or lousy) person?" "Does she pay her bills on time?" "Have you ever had to use a mechanic's lien to collect payment for work you did for her?" "Does she demand good work from her employees and subs?" You'll also want to be able to make sure that you have lien releases from all the subs.

Be sure to ask how long this particular subcontractor has worked for your prospective general contractor. If it has been only for a short time, ask the contractor which sub he or she used before and why the old subcontractor is no longer being used. Depending on how convincing the response is, you might want to check with the old sub to get the real story. Also, ask the subs whether they use their own crews exclusively. Again, you don't want your kids walking down a staircase that was built by an underpaid worker who doesn't speak the same language as the foreman.

The Suppliers

Your contractor has to get supplies from various sources—lumberyards, paint stores, plumbing-supply houses, and so on. They are usually well known by these businesspeople and often have credit accounts with them. Suppliers are, therefore, good sources as character and business references. You will, as in the case of subcontractors, want to ask questions about the prospective contractor's bill-paying patterns. You might want to ask which quality of supplies he or she tends to buy. A sink faucet can cost anywhere from $20 to $200, and if you fail to specify a particular model, you might get stuck with a piece of junk that will fail shortly after your contractor's warranty expires.

The Warranty

You will want assurances from contractors that they will guarantee their work and supplies. They must be willing to fully repair their work or replace it if it fails within a given period of time. One year is a bare minimum for normal wear and tear on anything but appliances. These usually carry the manufacturer's warranty, which might be for longer or shorter than a year. Roofing materials often come with a manufacturer's warranty, which could be as long as fifty years, depending on the type of roofing materials. Roofing contractors should be willing to guarantee the quality of their work for *at least* five years.

According to Linda Case of Remodeling Consulting Services in Silver Spring, Maryland, 96 percent of contractors go under within the first five years. A warranty means nothing if the warrantor skips town. She suggests that you do not have any major work done by a firm that has been in business for less than five years.

Tell the contractor that you want any manufacturers' warranties given to you before the job is completed. Without the written warranty and bill of sale for the appliance, you will not be able to enforce the warranty in case of product failure.

Insurance and Bonding

Contractors who do not carry workmen's comp (compensation) and liability insurance should be eliminated from consideration. Here's why.

Arleen and Jerry hire Don the contractor to add a bedroom to their house. Everything goes along fine until a worker who is employed by the roofing subcontractor falls off the roof and lands on a rake that is lying next to the house. The tines of the rake go through the worker's buttocks, causing severe muscle damage. He is laid up (not on his back since due to the nature of his injuries, he has to lie on his stomach) and hit with medical bills, loss of wages, and pain and suffering.

Several weeks after Arleen and Jerry pay off the contractor, they hear from the worker's attorney, who presents them with a claim for $10,000. Arleen and Jerry call the contractor, who tells them that he does not carry insurance. This means that there is no workmen's compensation coverage to pay for loss of wages and no liability coverage to pay for medical expenses and suffering. The couple is now faced with a dilemma: Do they pay up or do they go to court to try to prove that the general contractor and the roofer are at fault? Defending yourself in court is no pleasant experience. So either way, they lose.

So if the contractor doesn't carry insurance, don't tell him to leave your home and never look back. Just let him work up an estimate for you. You might as well benefit from any creative input (and a price comparison).

If the contractor claims to carry insurance, tell her that you will want to see proof of both workmen's comp and liability coverage before you sign a contract. If she balks, be very careful.

Written evidence of insurance is inadequate to prove that coverage is current. You want to be sure that contractors have not allowed coverage to lapse. You must call the insurance companies to be sure that the workmen's comp and liability insurance are still in force.

Many states require that contractors be covered by surety bonds, which pay off suppliers, subs, and customers who have been ripped off. California, for instance, has such a requirement, and you can check either with the bond insurer or the licensing agency to see if contractors hold such a bond. The limitation is that these bonds usually have small payouts. In California, a $5,000 bond is all that's required. If you are having a $50,000 job done, this gives you little assurance. And what if several suppliers, subs, and customers all make claims against the bond? Disaster!

Before you decide on an expensive job, ask whether the contractor will be willing to purchase a payment and completion bond. This is a bond which guarantees that any monies lost on the project or any additional expenses incurred because of the contractor's failure to complete will be paid to the homeowner. Bonding companies will not issue such bonds to contractors who cannot demonstrate financial stability.

Therefore, many contractors will not offer the option. This is a great way to find out if you are dealing with a remodeler who has a stable business. If your prospective contractor refuses to obtain a completion bond, ask yourself twice whether something might be wrong with the way he does business. Could he be robbing Peter to pay Paul? (When is this Peter guy going to learn to put a mechanic's lien on Paul's property in order to get his cash back?)

A completion bond is usually paid for by the homeowner. It runs in the neighborhood of 3 percent of the total contract price. But if you are having a $50,000 job done, isn't it worth an extra $1,500 to know that you won't get ripped off? Ask your lender to recommend or approve a bonding company.

Licenses

Refer to Appendix A to determine which type of licensing, if any, your state provides or requires for building contractors. In addition, you might want to confer with the department of consumer affairs in your city or county. Its regulations could compensate in areas in which your state is deficient. If you do reside in a state that requires licensing, make sure that you have contractors show you their licenses.

If the contractor doesn't carry his license, get the license number, write it down, and check it out later. I once had an upgrading job done on a rental unit. We chose a contractor who seemed competent. The price was right, and so were the terms. However, when I checked the license number with the California Contractors State License Board, I learned that it belonged to someone else. When I brought this to the attention of the contractor, he told me that he used to work for the license holder, who had retired and allows him to use the license. I wished him a nice life and looked for another candidate.

Licenses are important because they tell you that contractors meet at least the minimum standards for your state. In some states, that simply means that they paid a fee and filled out a form. But at least the license hasn't been suspended or revoked. In states that require testing, you are at least assured that licensees passed some sort of competency exam. However, in some states, like California, licensing agencies do not necessarily enforce their regulations seriously. California's Contractors State License Board, for example, is resistant to act upon complaints from consumers against licensed contractors.

I am not saying that there are no competent unlicensed contractors in states that require licensing. But you must ask, "Why are these people not licensed? What recourse will I have if they fail to perform properly? How can I check on previous complaints against them?"

In addition, you would be amazed to learn how many people are operating with licenses in fields other than the ones in which they are working. If the licensing in your state is specific for various areas of specialization, make sure that your electrician is not working with a carpenter's license.

Professional Organizations

Several organizations exist that give remodelers an extra appearance of professionalism. The contractors join for any of several reasons. Some feel that membership helps them keep on top of new developments in the industry. Others feel that showing the professional organization's logo is a way of impressing prospective customers. If the organization offers arbitration, this is an inducement for the customer in case a dispute arises between the parties. Ask the contractor candidates which professional organizations they belong to. Get the phone numbers and call the organizations. Ask them what pluses they have for you, the customer, and ascertain whether your prospective contractor is a member in good standing.

Two of the best-known organizations are the National Association of Home Builders (NAHB) and the National Association of the Remodeling Industry (NARI). These organizations provide their contractor members with information and education through newsletters or magazines from both the national organizations and their local chapters.

It is the objective of these professional associations to make their members better businesspeople. They do this largely through the local organizations. They believe that membership alone supplies a form of internal policing. According to a spokesperson for NAHB, it's hard to face your colleagues at a local gathering when there are outstanding complaints against you. Whether or not that is true, I do not know. But a contracting business that generates enough complaints against which it does not have adequate defenses is in jeopardy of losing its membership.

So although it is not essential that contactors belong to national or local professional organizations, it certainly is helpful to you to know if they do belong. You should also determine whether the remodeler has pledged to abide by the decisions of the organizations's arbitration program, if any. Such a program could provide you with a quick and inexpensive way to resolve disputes.

The question remains: How do you locate such organizations to find out if your prospective contractors belong—or to use them as a referring agency to contracting companies? Easy—just call contractor candidates and ask which associations they belong to. Then check with those organizations to see what services they provide and ask whether the contractors are members in good standing. You can also call the local office of the Better Business Bureau and ask about local professional organizations. The national office for NARI is at (800) 966–7601, and NAHB is at (800) 368–5242.

Other Factors

Call your local Better Business Bureau, your local department of consumer affairs, and your state licensing agency (if applicable) and ask whether your contractor candidate has any outstanding complaints against him. Do not skip this step. It could uncover a trail of nightmares that some contractors may have left in their wake.

Appearances can tell you a lot about a professional. Look the contractor over when he first appears at your door. Does he look like a slob (the possibility that he just came from working on a job site notwithstanding)? Does he present you with a professional business card? After his visit, walk him out to his vehicle. Does the interior look like it was hit by an indoor tornado, or is it clean and orderly? Some contractors work out of a business office; you might want to make up an excuse to drop by and see what the operation looks like. Does it look like a professional business or a fly-by-night operation?

Attitude is a factor that will definitely have an effect on your guts. Contractors who meet you with an uninterested, surly, or aggressive approach are telling you something: They are either uninterested, surly, or aggressive, and not someone whom you want to do business with or even have roaming around your house for a few weeks. If they would rather talk than listen to your suggestions or needs or if they are not able to respond directly to your questions, do you want them doing major construction in your home?

If, on the other hand, you are greeted by candidates who are patient, affable, interested, and responsive, you are on the right track. It does not necessarily mean that these people are right for the job, but at least you are eliminating the types who will definitely be hard to deal with.

Also, as you go around with the candidate and talk about what the job will entail, observe whether or not she takes notes in an orderly fashion on a pad. If the candidate doesn't do so, how reliable will her planning be?

Here is another important tip: Before you make a final choice, make sure that the addresses and phone numbers for the contractors are legitimate. Post office boxes, suite numbers, and telephone answering machines are often used to protect crooked businesspeople from ripped-off customers. Get a street address and check it out. Make sure that a human being is at the other end of the phone line for at least part of the day. And be sure that it's an actual employee of the company, not just someone who takes messages.

Architects

If you already have architectural plans, you must determine whether your prospect is willing to work with them. As I mentioned in Chapter 1, a contractor I know is resistant to working with someone else's plans because he usually finds them deficient for his purposes. He requires a substantial payment for his own architectural designer to look over the plans and adapt them before he will come up with an estimate. Some of the more sophisticated general contracting firms have their own architectural or design staffs. You must decide whether you want to use their architect's services or to go outside. So you must determine how well the contractor can work with the plans you present to her.

If you are planning a really large remodeling job—such as adding a second story or a new bed-and-bath suite—that might require the hiring of an architect, you will have to consult with the architect about the hiring of a contractor. Some architects have construction contractors in mind with whom they like to work. This may or may not be the best way to go. You will have to work it out with the architectural firm. They may be more than happy to simply draw up the plans and have you find your own contractor.

If an architect recommends a contractor, I advise you to do some comparison shopping. Without comparing, you're at the mercy of your architect and builder, especially if the cost of design and construction is combined into a single bill and contract.

Price

The cost of the job is one of the last considerations because it is the last piece of information you will get from the general contractor. And it's not always the most important aspect of your dealing with the contractor.

Example: Jerry and Arleen have whittled their candidates down to two choices, Connie's Contracting and Reginald's Remodeling. They are adding a nursery/child's bedroom to their ranch house. Both contracting companies have come in with similar overall plans. Connie came in with a price of $25,000. We join Jerry now while he is on the phone with Reginald:

". . . that brings the final price to $30,000," says Reginald.

"Oh, gee whillikers," says Jerry, "We really like dealing with you, but your price is just too high."

"What price did you get from your other contractor?" asks Reginald.

"Twenty-five grand."

"We would put three-eighths-inch plywood underlayment under the vinyl flooring. Was he gonna do that or use particle board—which swells when it gets wet?"

"I dunno."

"Our built-ins are all solid wood, custom built with corner turn-tables and indirect under-cabinet lighting. Are the others?"

"Uh . . ."

"You do remember that we install electrical outlets every six feet and prewire the ceiling above the ceiling panels so you can adapt your lighting as the child grows."

"Really?"

"Are the windows all solid wood, prefinished, double-paned with a tilt-in cleaning feature?"

"Uh . . . no," admits our hero weakly.

"I'll tell you what," says Reg, "I'll give you a ten-year warranty in writing on all structural work and I'll come down to $27,500. Whaddya say?"

In other words, make sure that you know what you are getting for the price. The extra money you spend may actually cost you less in the long run.

And if an offer seems too good to be true—it is. No one is going to give you something at a loss. Chapter 7 contains a story about a couple that started out adding on a second story for a price that was too good. If you must go for the too-good-to-be-true price, make sure that you insure yourself in every other way that I have recommended. Fair warning.

And don't forget to get the price quotes *in writing* along with all other facets of the job. Don't compare prices that are not in writing.

I strongly advise against the "time and materials" method of payment. It is a method whereby the work is paid for based upon how much time it takes. It allows contractors to slow their workers down in order to get more money out of you. And if they underestimate the cost of their labor expenses, you pay. And how can you keep track of how many hours each worker is putting in? You would have to know the salary of each worker and the number of hours each one puts in each day. Unless the job is simple *and* you're paying for just the contractor and an assistant *and* you are there to supervise the work, forget it. And even then, forget about it anyway.

Specialty Repair and Improvement Contractors

Most of the time when you call a contractor you are not seeking the services of a general contractor. Most often homeowners seek the services of either a repairperson or a specialty improvement contractor. The former are plumbers, electricians, plasterers, painters, handymen, and the like.

A specialized home improvement contractor might be a carpenter who builds decks or installs skylights, an electrician who installs lighting, or a flooring specialist. It makes sense that you would not call a general contractor to do such limited tasks.

It would be impossible for me to cover every type of home improvement specialist in every situation. I hope that you will be able to apply the following select samples to your individual situation.

Again, the best way to find a repair or home improvement specialist is by recommendation—not in the yellow pages. Let's start with the example of a plumber. In the nine years that I have been a homeowner, I have gone through six different plumbers. Some have not shown up when they were supposed to. Others padded their bills. One was a finagler; he seemed sincere but always found a way to overcharge. The only reliable plumbing company overcharges. But it's the only one I could count on for major repairs.

At one point I started using a separate company for drain clearing. This firm was reliable and much less expensive than using regular plumbers. I soon learned that it also employed people who perform regular repairs. And they showed up when they said they would. I now use both companies. For the routine repairs I use the drain-clearing outfit. For more sophisticated repairs and for plumbing installations I use the regular plumbing company.

It has been my experience that the large, multiple-location plumbers who offer extended days and hours of service for emergency service, who place huge advertisements in the yellow pages, and who advertise on television are not good choices. I cannot make an across-the-board generalization, because obviously I have not sampled them all. (Hey, I may know contractors, but I ain't God.)

In a rental apartment that I once owned with some friends, a pipe broke on a Sunday (I wished I was God for a day). I had to turn off the water for the entire four-unit apartment building. I was forced to call one of those high-profile plumbing-repair giants. The repairperson showed up and quoted me a price of more than $300 for a job that entailed the replacement of two short pieces of pipe and two or three connecting pieces. The job was completed in less than two-and-a-half hours. It was highway robbery. Unfortunately, I had no choice. It was a "yellow pages decision."

In short, choose specialists carefully. Learn from your mistakes and move on as soon as you know that the contracting professional is not reliable or fair.

When hiring a handyman (or handyperson?), a vinyl-flooring installer, and the like, it is not always practical to require a license. But when you are having plumbing or electrical work done, you must insist upon it if your state makes provisions for licensing. These are highly specialized tasks that must be done properly with the appropriate skills. The work is subject to local building ordinances and may require permits.

But let's say that you are having work done that falls in between the rigorous standards of plumbing and electrical on one end of the spectrum, and a handyman at the other end. Suppose that your plumber had to break open a wall and punch a few holes in your ceiling in order to replace some piping. You now have to find a suitable plasterer to patch the job up. You could risk calling a handyman, but plastering is an art. Matching the surrounding surface texture while not producing obvious ridges takes skill and practice. But there is no guarantee that a licensed plasterer will have those skills.

Your surest way of protecting yourself is to get recommendations from people you trust and to then consider price, attitude, and whether or not the plasterer is licensed. On occasion we have chosen unlicensed craftspeople because they were less expensive and easier to get hold of quickly.

A few years ago we decided to have a small deck built in our little backyard because our dog, who was a rescue job from the local pound, was tearing up the grass and making the yard look like a disaster area. The licensed carpenters we considered were astronomically expensive. We settled on someone who came highly recommended, had the right attitude (he felt right to our "guts"), and was reasonably priced. He did a beautiful job.

A year later we needed a fence built to confine our pooch. (It's amazing how expensive a free mutt can cost if it's neurotic enough.)

When we called the same carpenter back we found out that he had acquired a state license and that he had raised his fees considerably. We searched around and found someone through a referral service that we had used before. We settled on a struggling actor who makes his living in carpentry. His fee was low and he had to work around his audition schedule, but he delivered as promised.

At the small apartment house I owned with my partners, one unit's bathroom had a shower with plain walls. There was no tile to protect them, and so the walls were deteriorating. I referred to the magazine published by the local landlords' association. It carries hundreds of ads for all types of suppliers and repair professionals. We got estimates from a manufacturer of custom-molded wraparound wall covering, from a carpenter who installs walls, and from tile installers. All were licensed and expensive. Then I called my friendly referral agency, which sent over a fellow who had been working for someone else and had recently gone into business for himself. He was prompt and courteous, and he seemed to know what he was talking about. He explained how he would reinforce the walls, close the seams, apply the tile, and guarantee his work. He was unlicensed and inexpensive. He did the job quickly, neatly, and very well. I was happier than my dog when she's chewing a bone on her backyard deck.

Every situation is unique and presents its own problems. When choosing a craft professional (and make sure you choose a pro) approach each situation—whether it's a home remodeling job or a basic repair—with caution. Think creatively about different possible solutions and follow your gut feelings.

The Final Decision

Your final decision will be based upon all of the foregoing factors. You have eliminated those candidates without references, licenses (again, where applicable), business addresses and phones, a pleasant attitude, insurance, and all the rest. If there is more than one candidate left, you are at the point where you must make a decision.

At this point ask your remaining prospects for the job for itemized bids in writing. Look the bids over and compare what you are getting from the contractors. How good are the bids? Are they detailed? Are the supplies comparable? What is the difference in price? Is the higher price worth it? And don't forget your gut feeling. You are now ready to make your choice.

And here are two more tips:

1.   If you live in a metropolitan area, there may be a landlords' or apartment owners' association. Look them up and see if they issue any type of listing or publication that carries ads for professional contractors. Ask if they will send you a copy. It could be a great source of referrals to repair and building professionals. Those who list their services in such publications *should* be seasoned pros. And they should have lots of references.

2.   Don't hire amateurs. We once took the advice of a neighbor and had our house trim painted and repaired by his handyman. I describe this learning experience in the "Nightmare Alley" section of Chapter 7.

Things to Remember

1. You are entitled to demand what you want. Summon up the courage to be a tough negotiator. You are entitled to get what you pay for. Don't be intimidated into not demanding all the elements of a good deal. You hold the money, so you have the power. If the contractor doesn't see it that way, find another candidate.

2. Before deciding on a general contractor, know what you want. Have an idea of what you want in terms of changes, quality, price, and approximate design.

3. Let your guts be your guide. If you don't feel right about a contractor, your unconscious is telling you that something is wrong. Listen to it. Don't settle for less than you deserve.

4. Ask the contractor candidates for references. Call those references and ask questions. And visit the homes where the work was performed.

5. Make sure that the customer references had work done that required skills similar to the ones required for your project.

6. Ask many questions. Don't be afraid. Don't hold back. See page 20 for some basic questions.

7. Find out who the subcontractors are and ask them for references as to whether the contractor is reliable.

8. Ask who the contractors' suppliers are and contact them for references.

9. Make sure that the contractor is willing to guarantee her work and warranty the materials and that she will put this guarantee in writing.

10. Make sure that the contractor has been in business for at least five years.

11. Be sure that the contractor carries proper workmen's comp and liability insurance. Be sure that he carries a surety bond and—for big jobs—a payment and completion bond.

12. If your locale provides for licensing, ask to see the remodeler's license or get the number. Check to see that it is valid, current, for the proper specialty, and in the contracting company's name.

13. Find out which professional organizations the contractor belongs to and verify that membership.

14. Determine if the contractor is a current member of a professional trade organization and whether she has pledged to follow its operational guidelines.

15. Check with the Better Business Bureau, department of consumer affairs, and your local licensing agency (if applicable) to ask whether there are outstanding complaints against the contractor.

16. When you first meet contractors, take note of their appearance, attitude, and level of concern. These are very important.

17. If you are planning on using the services of an architect, determine how well the contractor you intend to use will be able to work with the architect, and vice versa. You may want to hire a contracting firm with a design department.

18. Don't consider only price. Check carefully to see what you are getting for your money. Sometimes extra charges cost less in the long run.

19. If you are using an architect, don't necessarily commit to that person's contractor until you have explored all options. Make sure that the contractor is willing to work with an outside architect's plans.

20. When looking for specialty contractors—such as electricians, plumbers, handymen, and the like—again, use a personal reference or a referral service.

21. Although a license is not essential for basic repairs, it is advisable to be cautious when hiring for jobs that require building permits or zoning compliance.

3

The Contract

After the destruction of Iraq that resulted from Operation Desert Storm, the Devil visited Saddam Hussein.

"I see you are in desperate need of reconstruction," observed the Prince of Darkness. "I am prepared to have the most amazing work crew assist you. They will completely rebuild Baghdad in one month and it will be more glorious than it has ever been before. In exchange, you must give me the souls of your grandchildren to burn in eternal hell."

"Hmmmm." Saddam Hussein thought for a moment. "What's the catch?"

YOU NEED NOT SELL YOUR KIDS' SOULS TO THE DEVIL IN order to get what you want from a contractor. Or for any negotiation in which the other party has to compete for your business.

Once you have decided on a general contractor, you're ready to go ahead with the project, right? It's a loaded question. Of course you knew that the answer is: not by a long shot. Not any more so, in fact, than initially picking a car dealer means that you will definitely be buying from that dealer. As a matter of fact, this could become the most grueling part of the enterprise if you're not on your toes. The bid that the contractor made is based strictly on an initial inspection of the job site and a superficial understanding of what your needs are. But now you have to negotiate the contract. This process requires thought, preparation, the right attitude, and patience.

During the course of making the contract for a major remodeling job you will become more specific about what you want as part of the deal. The contractor may decide that he or she wants more money in exchange. And so you might even want to lower your expectations to save some cash.

Once you notify the contractor that you have chosen her company, she should visit your home to go over the details. If she wants to do it all by mail, by fax, or over the phone, insist that it be done in person in your home. At the very least, this procedure, under the law, guarantees you the right to cancel within three days. In any case, it allows you to review sketches, drawings, blueprints, or whatever else will be necessary for your particular project. If you are dealing with the contractor's designer or with an outside architect you will want to review all technical drawings with the contractor. For the most part, I will be assuming that you followed the steps in Chapter 2 and that you will be dealing with a fairly reputable businessperson. The contractor will bring forms with her. The forms will be titled "Property Improvement Agreement" or something similar. But even if the remodeler merely has a pad, don't worry as long as you get a formal contract to sign when the deal is done. At this stage of the game you should be concerned only with getting everything down on paper.

The contractor should bring a copy of her original bid. Go over it with her and make sure it matches what you have on your copy (which should have been sent or presented to you). If you notice any discrepancy, rectify it immediately. Any such misunderstandings should be worked out and price adjustments made in writing. If you have had any changes of mind since the contractor's original inspection, discuss them now, before things get complicated.

For the purposes of illustration, I will discuss an improvement involving the addition of a second story that includes a bedroom for a child, a guest bedroom, a bathroom, and a wooden deck off the guest room. I am using this example because it covers many of the contingencies you are likely to confront. It doesn't cover some, but you should be able to apply these principles to almost any situation.

For such a drastic change in the structure of your home, you should definitely get a rendering of what the place will look like upon completion. This rendering should be included as part of your contract (this, incidentally, is why they're called "contractors"). You don't want to end up with a flat roof if you were envisioning a pitched one in your mind. If you used an architect to draw up the plans, he will provide you with such a picture as part of the proposal.

And never, never sign a contract with blank spaces. Always cross out any blank spaces when you are ready to sign. Spaces that are partially filled in should have their blank parts crossed out as well.

In short, the contract should contain everything. And when I say everything, I mean *everything*. Do you get it? Everything, everything, everything! E-V-E-R-Y-T-H-I-N-G For instance: "Bedroom #1—blue paint." Good enough? Does it contain *everything*? How about this?: "Bedroom #1—Walls to be painted with Benjamin Moore latex flat robin's egg blue. Sufficient number of coats to cover uniformly. All wood trim, doors, and window frames to be painted with Benjamin Moore antique white oil base satin enamel."

Here's a sample of electrical specifics. "Grounded (three-prong) double electrical outlets every eight feet. One quadruple outlet under center window. All outlets to be six inches above baseboard. Electrical outlet box to be installed in center of ceiling. Must be strong enough to bear weight of ceiling fan. Shmendrik brand eight-foot light track to be installed centered on ceiling three feet from north wall—no wires to be exposed. Customer will provide light fixtures for track."

How about the walls? Will there be insulation? What brand? What "R" rating (the rating measure for insulation)? Roll fiberglass or board insulation? And what will the interior walls be made of? Wood paneling? If so, what brand and style? Real wood planking or thin plywood covered with an imitation veneer? Or, probably, drywall (also called Sheetrock or plasterboard), which you will want to be five-eighths-inch thick unless you want an errant hammer to create extra ventilation later on when you hang pictures. $\frac{1}{2}''$ and especially $\frac{3}{8}''$ are too thin. All seams and nail heads should be made invisible under paint.

Now let's go to the bathroom. (You go first—I can wait.) First, let's list some of the areas you'll have to cover in your contract: porcelain fixtures, plumbing fixtures, pipes, cabinets, medicine cabinets, lighting, outlets, ventilation, mirrors, wall tile, flooring, doorknob and lock, paint, toilet paper holder (excuse me—bathroom tissue dispenser), towel bars. . . . I'll bet you didn't realize how much stuff there is to consider.

But remember, this book promises that you won't have to go through hell. Keep in mind that if you are adding a second story, you will be using either a highly skilled contractor whose company does complete design work, or you'll be using an architect. One of the advantages of using architects is that they will (or should) be keeping an eye on the remodeler to make sure that she is doing the job according to his specs. Just make sure that the architect has thought of everything that you will want in your plans. And keep in mind that architects do not necessarily pick out the paint, tile, towel racks, medicine cabinets, and the like. So what is missing from the architect's specifications will have to be provided by you.

When you sit down with the contractor to hash out the details you will, as a matter of course, have to start renegotiating price. This is because at this point you will get into the specifics of the job. You may not want standard plastic switchplates on your light switches. You like those fancy brass ones with the filigree work. The contractor was planning on Shmears brand Navajo white paint, and you decide that you just can't live without that expensive robin's egg blue I talked about . . . with contrasting trim. And you want the other bedroom done in golden blossom peach with the trim done in muted mauve. And although you do want the hallway done in Navajo white, you don't want the cheap Shmears paint. You want the good stuff.

As you go through the written agreement for a large job with the contractor, you will most assuredly be making more changes. You may decide that the bathroom counters should not be made of particle board covered with Formica or some other laminate. You want tile that matches the floor and wall tiles.

And you just saw a picture of a bathroom in *Better Homes and Gardens* with the most beautiful tile. You must have it. Unless you go out and buy the tile yourself and bring it home, you will have to pay the contractor for her time and trouble as well as for the increase in the cost of the tile. If the tile has to be laid in some unusual or sophisticated pattern, the cost of labor will rise as well.

Negotiating

My discussion of negotiating technique must be limited. It is a general subject that is, and has been, worthy of a tome of its own. (I almost never get to use the word *tome*.) But keep a general rule of mine in mind: Whoever holds the money has the power. What this means is that you are in a strong negotiating position if the other party wants your money and you are not in any immediate jeopardy if you withhold it.

Until you sign the contract, and even during the course of work, you are in a strong position to get much of what you want. You must, of course, be willing to let the other party walk away from the deal. Let's back up to the point at which you are ready to make the decision as to which contractor you will choose.

At this point I must refer you back to the Introduction, where I want you to go over The Rule of the Psychological Hump. You are now in one of the phases during which negotiating from a strong *emotional* position is important.

You have narrowed it down to two candidates, Bridgit and Woody. Bridgit thinks and communicates better than Woody. But her price for the second-story addition is $2,000 higher. So when she tells you her bid, you tell her that the other bid came in lower. She asks you by how much. And you tell her the truth: $3,500. Is this unethical? Not in my book. It is not likely that a party to a negotiation is going to take a job at a loss just to get the work. After all, she may have come in with a high bid just to see what she could get out of you. If she can come down to get the business, she will. And by telling her the differential is higher, you give her room to come down halfway—more or less.

If she says that she can't match the price, tell her that you will think it over and get back to her. You can wait a few days and call back. When you call back you can ask, let's say, for $1,000 off the price, ceiling fans in the bedrooms, and wallpaper in the hall in addition to the wallpaper in the kids' room that was part of the original bid. After all, the additional work for the electrician and for the paperhanger will not cost the contractor that much more. The wallpaper and the fans can usually be purchased for a modest additional cost to her. The variables are unlimited. And if Bridgit is unbending you can hire Woody. You have options. If you would like to make a study of negotiating techniques, I recommend *You Can Negotiate Anything* by Herb Cohen (Lyle Stuart, 1980).

Let's return to the present. You have chosen your contractor and are now deciding on changes and what they will cost before you sign the deal. Each time you mention an improvement or addition to the original specs you are likely to hear, "Okay, but that will cost you some extra money." You then ask how much, and the remodeler either says, "X dollars" or "I'll have to price it and get back to you." But is there anything you can do or say that will encourage the contractor to minimize additional cost, if not downright eliminate extra expense altogether? The answer is no if you don't negotiate. Let's use the paint as an example.

Jerry and Arleen are in the contract stage and tell Bridgit that they want Expensivo brand robin's egg blue paint in the guest room along with the Expensivo Navajo white trim. And they want peppermint pink walls in the kids' room and silly strawberry in the bath.

"That'll cost you a few bucks," says Bridgit.

"What's 'a few'?" asks Arleen.

"The paint will be about an extra $150, and the painter will probably cost an extra $350."

Jerry, who is drinking a beer, spits out a mouthful. "$350 *extra?*"

"It's a lot of trouble to change colors, what with changing the brushes between colors and having to use paint thinner to clean up the oil-base trim paint and having to mask the edges of the trim."

Arleen has an idea. "How about if you take the price of the original paint off the estimate? We'll buy the Expensivo paint and you get the painter to make the extra effort with our paint at no additional cost."

"I dunno," responds Bridgit.

"Well, think about it," Arleen says.

What happened here? In essence, everything was left in the air because Arleen is a brilliant negotiator and knows that other such small negotiations will go on as the parties progress through the specifications of the contract. There will be plenty of room for give and take over many of the remaining points of the agreement.

Keep in mind that you have not chosen a contractor for keeps until you sign the contract. And even then the deal ain't done. There's the three-day cancellation option. If you begin to show impatience at the remodeler's inflexibility, she should get the message that you still have other options—namely, other contractors. It is therefore a good idea when you first notify the contractor that she has won the job to let her know that it was a close choice between her and another candidate. The ghost of the other contractor will loom over your contractor's head during additional negotiations.

Let's look back on this chapter for a second. Keep in mind that you want everything in writing (I can't emphasize it enough). Remember that everything is negotiable. All elements of the work order may be played off against one another in working out compromises. You do not have go through with the deal if you are not satisfied with the way the negotiations are going. You can always choose another contractor. But that is a contingency you will want to avoid.

A few notes about negotiation attitude. Unless you are ready for various reasons to dump the contractor with whom you are negotiating, do not take an adversarial position. Be friendly and do not threaten the contractor—especially with the notion that you will choose another contractor if she doesn't give in. Hardlining doesn't help. You don't want to alienate the person who is going to be doing such an important job for you. Imagine what a position for revenge such an individual could be in. Besides, you don't want someone to take the job and then resent you. It makes for bad relations during construction, which in turn could make for a nightmare.

What Should Be in Every Contract

Again, *everything* should be in the contract. But we are not limited to supplies and labor when we discuss "everything." As I mentioned before, warranties are included. Vitally important too are these elements:

- ☑ The date the agreement is signed.
- ☑ Your name and address.
- ☑ The contractor's name and address. And be sure that you get a street address and check it out to make sure it's valid.
- ☑ The contractor's license (if applicable) or registration number.
- ☑ Location of the job site if it's different from your home address.
- ☑ A copy of all detailed drawings, blueprints, sketches, and specifications.
- ☑ The name of the person who will supervise the project on a daily basis. You will probably want the general contractor's name here.
- ☑ A statement holding the contractor responsible for obtaining all necessary permits and inspection approvals.
- ☑ Anything the contractor vows, asserts, promises, pledges, guarantees, warrants, avers, denotes, or agrees to.
- ☑ Starting dates for various aspects of the job.
- ☑ Completion dates.
- ☑ Model numbers of appliances. (Some experts recommend that you include the phrase "or equivalent" after the model number, or that you specify alternate models. I don't. Who is to determine what "equivalent" is, and why give contractors carte blanche to use your second choice when all that's needed for them to find your first choice is a little extra footwork?)
- ☑ Cleanup procedures, both during the job and upon completion (you don't want your property to be a mess at the end of each workday).

☑   The payment schedule (more about this to follow).

☑   Waivers of mechanics' liens.

☑   Insurance.

☑   Payment and performance (also referred to as payment & completion) bonds or the use of a funding control company (refer to page 84).

☑   Late-completion penalties.

☑   Responsibility for: building permits, compliance with zoning and building regulations and government inspections. (All building permits shall be applied for by contractors in their own names.)

☑   Finally, if you are planning on doing some of the work—or if you intend to hire someone besides the contractor to do it—*you must so specify in your contract*.

Warranties

A word about warranties: *excellent*. Aah, what the heck, here are a few more words: Read and understand them as well as any other part of your contract. The warranty should be fully spelled out. It should state whether it covers labor, parts, or both—and for what period of time. As with almost every other warranty, labor is usually the most cost-intensive part of a repair. The cost of the lumber for repairing a cabinet shelf is just a couple of bucks. But the cost of a carpenter to make the repair can be very high. It is labor that you most want to have covered. Is the warranty limited or unlimited? That is, does it cover full cost for any and all failures of workmanship, or does it have limitations as to what it covers and as to financial limitations such as deductibles? (A deductible is an initial amount that the customer must pay before the warranty takes effect.)

No warranty should be for less than one full year of unlimited coverage for materials *and* labor. Some contractors may be willing to extend that limitation if you negotiate for it. Or they may be willing to offer you an extended warranty at a reasonable price. An extended warranty, as in the case of automobiles, is essentially an insurance policy that is put out by a private company. It insures you against costs for repairs during a certain period. Some remodelers will offer them as part of their service in order to attract customers. One such warranty policy is offered by Home Owners Warranty (HOW). The HOW Remodeler Program enlists contractors who it feels have technical ability, financial security, and offer customer service.

Here, in a nutshell, is the way remodeling warranty companies work. HOW guarantees all work for one year. Through the second year it backs all major systems and structural work. Through the fifth year it guarantees all structural work. Some contractors can even offer a ten-year structural warranty. When you get a HOW warranty, or a similar one offered by another company, you are receiving backing by a company apart from the contractor. In this way you can avoid disputes with the remodeler after the job. HOW also offers a dispute-settlement service. And the warranty stays with the house even if you move—a good selling point. I am not endorsing any particular program. An outside warranty is an option that you should bring up with a contractor. If she participates in a warranty program, make sure that it is so stated in the contract and that you receive a copy of the warranty.

Sanitation

If you are having a job done that will leave only one toilet accessible to your family and do not want laborers traipsing through your home to relieve themselves, you may want to include provisions for sanitation facilities on the job site.

Payment Schedule

The payment schedule is a simple part of the negotiating process, but it becomes tricky as well. The contractor will want a deposit up front so that she can purchase your materials and supplies at your expense. Fair enough. After that she will want payments to be made according to a schedule. Each payment is usually timed to proportionately correspond with the amount of time that has passed since the project started (assuming the project is proceeding according to schedule).

Unless you are involved in a mammoth undertaking, 5 to 10 percent should be a reasonable down payment made upon the signing of the contract. After that, the number and amount of payments should reflect your willingness to pay as you go and contractors' needs to get their bills paid and their labors rewarded.

Here is a sample from an actual kitchen remodeling job:

PAYMENT SCHEDULE

$ 500	Down payment
2,673	Day job starts
2,673	Upon completion of rough electrical

2,673	Upon delivery of cabinets
1,500	Upon completion of job
1,176	31 days after completion

Notice that the contractor asked for less than a 5 percent down payment and for a little less than 25 percent upon commencement of work—a perfectly acceptable variation. And he was willing to leave a similar amount unpaid until actual completion of the job.

Keeping the Work on Schedule

If you have an important reason to keep the project on schedule and have it completed by a specific date, include in the contract language which says that "time is of the essence." Indicate that delays will constitute a breach of the contract and that failure to complete on time will require compensation to the owner according to the daily penalty under "substantial completion."

The compelling factor to make time of the essence has to be serious. You can't just say, "My spouse will nag me if the job isn't finished on time" if you want a judge to enforce penalties against the contractor. But if you are selling the property because you must move, if your Eastern European relatives are coming to live with you in the new world or if bitter cold weather is looming, you have good reason to claim that time is of the essence. Thereby, if "substantial completion" is achieved on time there will be no reason to seek penalties. A "time is of the essence" clause helps to enforce the substantial-completion requirements of the contract.

Substantial Completion

In the previous paragraph I referred to "substantial completion." What this roughly translates to is that the job is finished except for some of the fine points. It means that the improved area is essentially usable for the purposes for which it was intended. A roof missing from a bedroom indicates that the job has not been substantially completed. The same holds true for a toilet bowl missing from the toilet. However, wrong faucet handles in the bathroom or an uninstalled light fixture in the bedroom do not preclude substantial completion. The rooms in the latter examples would still be fully usable. Cases in between these extremes might have to be evaluated by an arbitrator or judge. But none of these examples would qualify for fulfillment of the contract as would warrant full final payment. A judge or arbitrator could order you to pay up *minus* the cost of having the job completed by an outside professional.

You will want in the contract a clause that sets a date for substantial completion and that levies penalties for failure to complete on time. This may be different from the date of payment because although you can live without final completion, you cannot live without substantial completion if the bedroom walls and roof aren't finished when your relatives arrive from Europe in January. The clause should read something like this:

> All work done under this contract shall be substantially completed by _____ , 199__ . Failure to complete by such date will entitle owner to deduct $ _____ per day for each day's delay beyond such date. The date of substantial completion may be changed subject to authorized time adjustments signed by owner and contractor.

This clause serves as an inducement to the contractor to get the job done on time. Of course, change orders that delay the work should allow the contractor extra time to complete (sounds sort of sexual). You will have to get the contractor to agree to the inclusion of the clause, the date, and the daily rate. She may already have set such a rate that you may either negotiate or accept.

Liens and Waivers

According to *Black's Law Dictionary*, a mechanic's lien is "a claim created by law for the purpose of securing priority of payment of the price or value of work performed and materials furnished in erecting or repairing a building or other structure, and as such attaches to the land as well as buildings and improvements erected thereon." Huh? What this means is that if someone supplies you with labor or materials that become part of your home, the supplier has a claim against your property. And if you fail to pay the claimant the amount due, that person can either sue you or stop the sale of your home until you pay the debt. And what happens if you are successfully sued but you can't afford to pay the judgment? The suing party might be able to foreclose and force a sale of your property in order to pay off the lien claim. Sound like a nightmare? Welcome to the Twilight Zone.

Now let's complicate the picture and make it relevant to this book. Let's say you pay a contractor who then hires subs and orders materials to make improvements to your property. And then he fails to pay them. The suppliers and subs then make an effort to get their money from the contractor, but he moved to Hawaii. (If you are reading this book in

Hawaii, the contractor moved to Alaska.) The claimants, having nowhere else to turn, turn in the direction of your home. They notify you that they have placed liens on your property. Can you prevent this? Almost.

Each time you pay the contractor after the initial payment you will need a "lien release" or "waiver of mechanic's liens" from each sub and supplier. The procedure will be discussed in Chapter 5, but *you must provide for it in the contract*. It could save your bank account or even your home. The language of the provision should approximate this:

> At each payment made by owner to Contractor, the Contractor will provide to Owner acknowledgment of payment from each supplier and subcontractor as well as from the Contractor for all materials, equipment, and labor provided by the date of the previous payment. Upon final payment, the Contractor will provide waivers or releases of payment from all suppliers, subcontractors, and from the Contractor.

This requires contractors to provide you with an "Acknowledgment of Payment" whenever you make an installment payment according to your payment schedule. You will have proof that the suppliers' and subs' bills have been paid. If the contractor balks at having to go through all of the trouble each time she collects payment, you must insist upon it. *It should not be a negotiable issue.* Remember, however, that we are not talking about small improvements here. The installation of a new kitchen sink does not prudently require all this, but the addition of an entire kitchen merits extra safeguards.

Funding Control

"Funding control" refers to the disbursement of payments during the project. Obviously, payments must not be paid willy-nilly (whatever the heck that means). You want the payments to be controlled in such a way that you are guaranteeing that you will not be ripped off and that you will not be stuck with any mechanics' liens when the job is finished. There are three basic ways of controlling funding:

1.   controlling payments yourself
2.   using a *joint control* company
3.   having your lender control payments.

Controlling Payments Yourself

If you control disbursements yourself, no particular stipulation need be made in the contract, unless the contractor asks for it. The process involved in doing this will be covered in Chapter 5.

Joint Control Companies

If you are doing an expensive home improvement job you may find it worthwhile to locate a joint control—or funding control—company to oversee the job. For a fee, such a company takes the money for the project and holds it in an account. As the job progresses, it issues payments to the suppliers and subcontractors directly as well as to the general contractor. In essence, joint controls are escrow companies.

The funds for the project are put into an account. As each part of the project is completed, the contractor issues vouchers to the suppliers and subs for their input into the job as of a specific date. The suppliers and subs send the vouchers to the joint control company, which issues them payment. Along with the vouchers, they present to the "joint control" invoices and receipts that serve as evidence of the work or materials supplied to the project.

Sometimes the joint control will send an inspector to the job site to see that things are progressing and that material is being delivered as per the contract. Note that such inspectors are normally there for no other purpose. They do not evaluate the quality of the work or materials. You must read your joint control agreement carefully to understand the extent of what the company guarantees.

I strongly recommend this type of payment control for any large job. What constitutes a large job will vary depending on the cost of living where you reside, but any project costing $25,000 or more should qualify. Many general contractors will balk at the idea of having to do the extra work involved to satisfy the criteria of a joint control, but a reputable firm should concede if you insist. A contractor friend of mine whose ethics are of the highest caliber actually prefers being paid through a joint control company because he feels that there will be no doubts on the part of his customers and his suppliers about the way he is conducting his business. He knows that if *he* prefers the most businesslike and professional ways of doing business, his customers will be happy.

What are the drawbacks of using a funding controller? It will cost you a few percentage points more to get the job done, and you may end up with some cranky subcontractors at your job site who don't want to bother with getting vouchers redeemed. The latter issue is not really your problem. As to the extra cost, look at it this way: On a $30,000 job for which you have to pay a 3 percent fee, the total cost will increase by $900. Not much of a jump in price to take the pressures of monitoring the job off your mind (for the most part). Think of the extra sleep you'll get for the months that the job will be going on. Think of how much less you'll have to worry about mechanics' liens from suppliers you never knew existed.

How does one find a joint control company? That, again, depends upon where you live. Start with the contractor herself. She may know of a firm with which she has worked successfully before. If you are financing the project through a lender, that institution should be happy to help you find one—it's in its best interest. (Have you ever heard of a lender that doesn't want as many types of assurance as it can get before it lends you money on your home that it could just as easily invest in junk bonds and international speculation?) Even if you are not borrowing to finance the project, you could ask your friendly neighborhood banker to recommend someone.

Once you locate a funding controller, check out the company with your state banking department and your local Better Business Bureau. You don't want to trust your money to Vito's Joint Control and Drain Cleaning Company just because the contractor says to. You want to know that it has a track record and that it hasn't filed for Chapter 11 bankruptcy. Vito could take your money and spend a year lounging in Ipanema.

To find your state banking authority, call your state representative's office and ask for the number.

Lending Institutions

Some lenders are now requiring joint control by which they themselves disperse the loan funds directly to the contractor, the subs, and the suppliers. They save the expense of an outside joint control company and, perhaps, pass the savings onto you. You never receive the funds—they go directly from the bank to your creditors. A neat and tidy package. The contractor has no choice but to accept the deal or walk. If she walks, she probably wasn't worth doing business with.

Change Orders

Let's say that work has begun on your new second-story addition and that you change your mind about some of the specifics. It's almost certain that you will.

Example: Arleen and Jerry's second-story addition is going along swimmingly. Everything looks good, and the work is right on schedule. The contractor is ready to start on the bathroom interior on Monday. But here it is, Friday morning, and our hero and heroine have just come across tiles that depict *The Wizard of Oz*. They tell the contractor about it, and he agrees to have the tiles changed. "Great," says Jerry. "I've got to get to work. See ya later."

"Not so fast," responds the contractor. "We have to change the contract."

"Excuse me?" says Arleen.

Connie the Contractor explains: "The price of the tiles will go up dramatically. You want very expensive stuff. Plus, because it has to be installed in a very specific pattern, the cost of installation will go up as well. The tiler will have to return the present tile and then go to the dealer who carries the new tile. This could delay the job by a couple of days. So we have to adjust the contract for materials, costs, and the completion date." Is the contractor right? You bet she is. It is time for a "change order." (Hence the title of this section.)

Contractors are not likely to get involved in a more expensive addendum to the project without protecting themselves. And the same wisdom applies to wary customers. Your contractor should have forms for this purpose. If not, make up your own. Be sure each change order includes:

- The date of the change agreement
- The project you are referring to
- A description of what is being added and deleted and a full description of materials and services to be added
- Additional charges (or a reduction of charges—hey it *could* happen!)
- Completion date change
- Signatures of all parties

Change orders become part of the contract and thereby fit within the parameters of "everything" when I warn you to get *everything* in writing.

Financing Contingency

If you require outside financing in order to pay for a remodeling job, your contract should contain a provision that makes the contact voidable on the part of the homeowner in the event that you are unable to obtain a loan at a specified rate for a specified period of time.

If you are hiring a contractor for damage repair that is covered by insurance, determine how much expense your insurer is going to cover before you sign the contract.

Hours of Work and Noise Levels

If you live close to your neighbors, and who doesn't—(okay, so you happen to be a farmer and I'm a dumb city slicker)—you don't want them hating you. And if you live in an urban or suburban neighborhood, you can bet that at least one neighbor sleeps late. So unless you're trying to get even with one of them, make sure that a daily start time is mentioned in your contract. I personally set 8:00 A.M. so that my neighbors don't have to hear power saws first thing in the morning. (It's also a good idea to alert your neighbors before work commences—it could smooth a lot of ruffled feathers.)

If you don't want to breathe wood dust and hear the din of power tools when you return from a stressful day of work, you might want to specify a daily finish time as well. And don't forget to negotiate days of work. Contingent on local ordinances, your contractor might want to have access to your home on weekends. Such issues should be included in the contract unless you won't mind a roofer knocking nails in over your head at 7:00 A.M. on Sunday.

Cleanup

You can count on three things in life: death, taxes, and a messy home during remodeling. But you can cut down on the amount of mess while construction is going on simply by putting some basic cleanup requirements in the contract. Remodelers should be agreeable as long as the restrictions are reasonable. Depending on the nature of the job, a paragraph like the following should set some reasonable limits:

> At the end of each workday the work site shall be cleaned as follows: Dirt, dust, scraps, and debris shall be removed from the area to a practical extent, particularly with regard to the living spaces adjacent to the place of actual improvement work. Tools shall be stored safely in an area to be approved by the owner. All materials shall be neatly stored out of harm's way to the degree feasible. In the event that such cleanup is not done, owner shall reserve the right to deduct $50.00 per

day for each incident after once alerting the contractor to an initial such omission.

Even if the contractor refuses to agree to such a penalty stipulation (can you blame her?) she will at least be aware of how serious you are about keeping your home moderately clean.

The contract should stipulate that at the end of the project the job site must be left broom clean and all debris must be removed.

Final Payment

Substantial completion aside, you should always reserve as much of the payment as possible until *full completion* of the work. This includes full completion of all work under this contract as well as passing all necessary inspections by the proper authorities *as well as by the owner*. That last clause may not sit well with the contractor but tell her that you just want to make sure that the work is satisfactory *to you* before handing over the final payment. If you are contracting a very large job with four or more payments, make sure that the payment schedule includes a *substantial-completion* payment as well as a final-completion payment. Again, that last payment must be significant enough to make it well worth the contractor's while to see that everything is done in a satisfactory manner. Five percent just won't cut it—try to set it at 25 percent or more. But I strongly advise that you do not go below 15 percent unless the contractor is your own mother. And I'm not so sure about her. Remember, if the contractor perceives you as a big pain in the neck (does anyone say that phrase with that part of the anatomy anymore?) and it's busy season, she may just decide to forget about finishing the job to your finicky specs if it means a mere $3,000 loss on a $30,000 job.

As we discuss mechanics' liens, you will realize how important it is that you protect your home from such liabilities. And one of the surest ways to assure this protection is to include in the payment schedule a provision which says that the final payment will be made only after the period for notifying you of mechanics' liens has passed. In California, subcontractors and suppliers have thirty days from the completion date of the remodeling project to notify the owner of their intention to make a lien claim for unpaid bills. After thirty days they lose that right and must seek redress in law from the general contractor. You should consult your state consumer regulatory agency for the preliminary notice filing period where you live. Use that period as the retention period before final payment is made after completion.

Arbitration

It is usually better to have contract disputes settled in an arbitrator's office than in a courtroom. Courts can get pretty ugly (especially if they're old and dingy) and troublesome. You are in an adversary situation, rife with bitterness and resentment of the first order. You could get involved in legal costs and wasted time. Arbitration provides that both you and the other party will have your dispute settled by an arbitration service that you designate in the contract. Most commonly, the American Arbitration Association (AAA) is selected in preprinted contracts. Although it is well known and highly respected and has vast experience in contractor-related disputes, some people feel that the AAA tends to lean in favor of businesses. If you know an attorney, ask him or her to recommend another arbitration service. Many county bar associations across the country offer mediation services—often at no charge. You can call yours and ask about arbitration services. Look under your county bar association in the white pages.

If the job is being covered by a warranty company, you may opt to use that company's arbitration services. You may also use arbitration services offered by the professional trade association to which your contractor belongs. However, it would be wise for you to research this option thoroughly before using it. How likely is it that a professional contractors' association would favor the customer? Before you sign a contract that requires such arbitration, contact the association and ask for access to its files so that you can randomly select cases, call the customers involved, and ask them how they feel about how the cases were handled. Don't call only customers who won their disputes. See how the losers felt about the conduct of the arbitration sessions. Sound like too much work? Then forget about using a trade association.

If the contract doesn't already contain language for dispute settlement, it should be added. The language should read something like the following:

> All claims and disputes between the parties that relate to this contract shall be resolved by arbitration that shall be provided by _____ unless the owner and contractor mutually agree to resolve them by other means.

Some printed contracts contain language that limits the contractor's damages to the cash price of the contract. Eliminate any such provision. Why? I'm glad you asked. Let's say that you are having your kitchen remodeled. One of the workers accidentally leaves a gas-supply pipe open and departs for the evening. You arrive home a few hours later and flick on the light switch. A tiny spark is ignited inside the switch and . . . *kaboom!* You wake up in the hospital the next day. You'll be okay in a week, but your house now looks like Dresden at the end of World War II. Do you think the contractor's liability should be limited to the $10,000 cost of remodeling your kitchen?

Owner's Right of Supervision and Inspection

The contract should include a statement that establishes your right to supervise and inspect the work being done even though the printed contract may have a provision that defines the contractor's control over the job. You don't want the job to get away from you if you have reservations about the way things are going. It should contain the following provision:

> Notwithstanding other provisions in this contract, the work in progress under this contract must meet the approval of the owner and shall be subjected to the owner's inspection and supervision in order to guarantee his (her, their) satisfaction.

If the contract contains other language that guarantees the contractor's control over how the project will be completed, this provision preserves your right to stick your "two cents' worth" in. It is actually to the advantage of both parties to have this language. Later on if something is wrong, this clause may protect the contractor. On the other hand, your voice during the course of the project may head off a disaster.

This added provision simply clarifies your right to stay involved and express your feelings and opinions while the job is moving ahead. The contractor may not listen to you, but because of other provisions in the contract he or she must ultimately get your approval on the completed job. Forewarned is forearmed. (Now I get what that means.)

Cancellation and Termination

Don't sign a home improvement contract anywhere but in your home. Federal law as administered by the Federal Trade Commission requires that when a contract is entered into at your home the contractor must provide you with a cancellation form and information about your cancellation rights at the time you sign the contract. This form empowers you to cancel the contract within three days of your signing it. If the contractor fails to provide you with the form, add the following words to the contract:

> Owner reserves the right to cancel this contract within three
> days of signing.

The reason for the law is that many innocent people have been fast-talked by home improvement salespeople into signing ridiculous contracts that have left homes in shambles with the owners having paid the unscrupulous companies large amounts of money. (See Chapter 7 for examples.)

Whenever you cancel or terminate a contract, do so in writing. Either send a telegram or a certified letter with return receipt requested. You want to have proof that you notified the contractor.

In the event that the work is progressing in a way that is completely unacceptable to you (e.g., a workman killed your cat; the place is left a shambles every day; the rain got into the house through the open roof and destroyed half your furnishings and your grandmother's heirloom rug), you will want a way out of the contract. And you might want a recourse for damages as well. HALT, the legal reform organization, recommends that this clause be included in your contract:

> Owner may end this contract if the contractor's work is
> unsatisfactory. All disagreements over payments due and ow-
> ing will be resolved in arbitration as provided.

Any contractor with half a brain will want to add a reciprocal clause that protects her from late payments and unbearably overbearing and capricious supervision on the part of the owner. That would be fine as long as such a clause is narrowly defined and doesn't allow for the contractor to walk away for some arbitrary reason or because of a bad-faith whim.

Purchasing Appliances

It is usually a good idea for you to supply consumer appliances on your own and have the contractor install them. Most such appliances are those connected with kitchen improvements but may also include outside-mounted central air conditioners, surface-mounted lighting fixtures, free-standing fireplaces, and even basic toilet bowls or bathroom sinks. There are several reasons.

First, contractors will usually charge you retail plus a fee for the effort they make to purchase and deliver the materials. You may have more time than they to look around for the best bargains.

Second, contractors may not be as painstaking as you in locating the most aesthetically pleasing models or those with all the best features. (Shopping for top-of-the-line refrigerators now would be greatly helped by a degree in thermodynamics and/or trigonometry.) You may want to peruse copies of *Consumer Reports* and similar publications before deciding on what to purchase.

Third, you may be able to extend the warranties on appliances by as much as a year at no additional expense to you. Most issuers of "gold" credit cards offer programs that double the manufacturers' warranties for a period of up to one additional year if you purchase a product with such a card. If you don't have one of these cards, I strongly recommend that you get one. All you need is a good credit record. Several card issuers even charge no annual fees. A list of such cards is available from Bankcard Holders of America, at 800-553-8025. By charging the appliance purchases and paying the credit card bill immediately, you double the warranties (up to one year) without any additional cost.

What's the catch? You must coordinate with the contractor for the appliances to arrive in time at the job site. The carpenter cannot build cabinets and a counter around a dishwasher that isn't there to be installed. The same holds true for the washer, dryer, refrigerator, oven, range, microwave oven, garbage disposal, and so on. If you can take the time and trouble, you can save money, get exactly what you want, and extend the warranties.

If you do decide to purchase your own appliances, stipulate in the contract which appliances you will be providing.

Specialty Contractors or Subcontractors

There are those jobs that are not large enough to require the services of a general contractor. But they're too big to trust to a handyman or to your pal Sid. For example, you need to replace the worn-out old-fashioned tub in your bathroom or want a deck built in your yard adjacent to the den. You're not in the mood to get bogged down in all of the details of a contract as I just described. On the other hand, the work will still be fairly extensive. What's the best way to handle it?

First, familiarize yourself with all the stuff I've thrown at you in this chapter. The more you have a sense of how these things work, the easier it will be for you no matter what the variations. Jobs like these involve considerable time, work, and expense, and so you still need to protect yourself. So once you have selected an outfit to do the job, tell it you want a detailed written contract. If it says that it has no idea where to get one or how to write one, volunteer to arrange it.

You can either write a contract in simple language or purchase blank contract forms. Office-supply and stationery stores carry these blank contracts. If you cannot find forms, you can send away for them. One of the major legal-form companies is Wolcotts, which you can call toll free at (800) 262–1538 or write to at 214 South Spring Street, Los Angeles, CA 90012. Remember, you may add to, or delete from, the forms as you please. Just be sure that in each instance you initial the change and have the contractor do the same. Both copies of the contract should be identical.

Wilhelm Publishing of Columbia, Missouri, puts out a contract kit that covers all the types of major remodeling agreements and many of the variations and alterations you are likely to deal with.

Try not to pay for anything in advance. However, it would not be unreasonable for contractors to ask for payment in advance to purchase materials. But don't make such a payment unless you first have a signed contract. Just as the contractor doesn't want to get stuck with a thousand dollars' worth of lumber because you change your mind after she buys the materials, you don't want to get stuck with an empty bank account because she used the money to buy lumber for another job that she had underestimated and after which she will be taking an extended vacation in Rio.

Of course, a dishonest contractor can sign a contract, take your money, and still disappear. Another way to protect yourself is to offer to meet the contractor at the material supplier and to pay for the materials right there. It is, of course, possible to insult contractors by implying that you don't trust them, but that's their problem. The best you can do is try to be diplomatic.

Generally, painters are hired without written contracts. The usual procedure is a verbal (oral) agreement or a simple written estimate on an estimate form. However, I strongly advise that unless you are having just one room painted one color with a common brand of paint, you have a written contract. Specifics regarding brands of paint, particular colors and finishes, plastering, spackling, contrasting colors for walls and trim, moving of furniture, responsibility for keeping paint off flooring and furniture, completion dates, and the like should all be written out. This eliminates misunderstandings and disputes. On the other hand, you don't necessarily need every detail written out as you would with a major home improvement.

A simple plumbing repair right there while you're watching does not usually warrant a contract. The same is true for the addition of an electrical socket, the replacement of a window, or the laying of new vinyl kitchen flooring. What you must consider are the size of the job, the reputation of the people performing it, how long they have been in business, and other basics such as proof of insurance and a license.

The more expensive or complex the job, the more you will want to consider including the following stipulations in your contract:

> Should Contractor damage the work of others or damage existing structures or items, he or she must repair the damages at his or her own expense or pay for such repair.
>
> Contractor shall obtain all necessary permits in order to perform work according to applicable regulations.
>
> Contractor is responsible for paying his or her own workers without those workers' having any claim against Owner.
>
> Contractor guarantees his (or her) work for [fill in a period of time].

Also, consider including language about arbitration in case of disputes on costly jobs.

Things to Remember

1. Don't be afraid to negotiate the fine points of the contract with the remodeler.

2. Don't let a preprinted form intimidate you. Everything in the contract is negotiable except for terms required by law.

3. As the contractor writes out the terms of the contract, go over your list to make sure that no points are overlooked and that you bring up any additions or changes you are considering.

4. For jobs that require substantial renovation, make sketches or building plans a part of the contract.

5. You cannot have too much detail in a contract. Put in as many specifications as you can think of.

6. For major remodeling jobs, consider having designs done by an architect. But try to determine whether the remodeler you want will be able to work with the architect's plans, whether the architect can recommend contractors with whom he or she can work and who offer competitive bids, or whether you can find a contractor who has adequate design services.

7. If you decide to work with an architect and a remodeler, make sure that all of your needs appear in the remodeler's contract, as the architect will not necessarily cover all of the accessories and other decorative details.

8. Remember, whoever holds the money has the power. You can negotiate for upgrades in your remodeling job or a reduction in price before you put your name on the dotted line. But don't push it.

9. You can, if you are willing to be calculating, use the specter of another contractor waiting in the wings as a bargaining chip to help you negotiate with the contractor of first choice.

10. Try to get as extensive as possible a warranty from the contractor. Most desirable is a warranty insurance policy offered by a well-established issuing company.

11. If necessary, include a provision for sanitation facilities for workers.

12. Include a start date and a completion date along with a payment schedule based on phases of the job being completed. Include financial penalties for late completion.

13. Establish with the remodeler that you must have the job substantially completed by a certain date. To support the substantial-completion provision, include a "time is of the essence" clause.

14. Include provisions for workmen's compensation and liability insurance as well as for a completion—or performance—bond.

15. Include provisions for ensuring that the contractor provides you with lien releases and proof of payment to subs and suppliers to protect you from liens on your property.

16. Consider a joint control company for keeping an eye on the project through the control of funds paid to the contractor, suppliers, and subs. If you are using outside financing, your lender may offer such service.

17. Make sure that there are clear provisions for changing the work or materials desired for the job. These should include procedures for determining updated costs and adjusted completion dates.

18. Include stipulations for work hours and days.

19. Work out with the contractor how clean the job site will be left at the end of each day. Include this language in the contract.

20. The contract should specify that when the job is completed the site will be left "broom clean" and that all waste and debris will be removed and disposed of in accordance with local ordinances. (You don't want paint poured down the drain or dumped with the trash, thereby poisoning the environment.)

21. Specify that final payment will be made only after full completion of the job, including inspection by the owner and by proper authorities.

22. Try to make the amount of the final payment as large as possible.

23. Stipulate that a substantial final payment to the contractor will occur only after the period has passed during which subcontractors and suppliers may file notices of mechanics' liens.

24. Make sure that the contract includes that disputes will be settled through arbitration. Do some research and determine which agency you will use for arbitration.

25. Include a clause that entitles you to inspect and supervise the job as work progresses.

26. Include a clause that entitles you to terminate the job in the event of poor performance by the contractor.

27. Include language which states the legal requirement that the contract can be canceled within three days (provided that the contract is signed at your home).

28. Consider purchasing appliances on your own in order to save money and to get exactly the features you want.

29. When dealing with specialty contractors, let the individual circumstances determine whether you need a detailed contract. More expensive or complicated jobs should be protected by a contract.

30. If the contractor does not have a contract form, either write one yourself or purchase a blank form and alter it to fit your needs.

31. Try not to pay any sums in advance. If you must pay for materials in advance, use a contract and/or pay for the materials directly to the supplier.

4

Financing the Project

Robert Benchley, the great American humorist, applied to his bank for a loan. The loan was immediately approved without restrictions. Benchley wrote back to his bank and closed his account there, saying, "I don't trust a bank that would lend money to such a poor risk."

YOU MAY NOT HAVE THE CASH AVAILABLE TO FINANCE A major home improvement project. This, of course, means that you will have to borrow the money or get the contractor to do the work on credit. And unless he or she is a relative, a close friend, or extremely stupid, this is highly unlikely. You need to find a home improvement lender who will give you the best deal.

Lending Institutions

Banks and mortgage lenders are usually the first places that people go to borrow money—and for good reason. They have lots of it, or at least they did until about 1990. There are several ways to borrow from a bank. One is to borrow against the equity in your home by taking a second trust deed, or second mortgage (or a first mortgage, if your home is paid for). A home equity loan is a variation of such a second trust deed. If you already have a second trust deed on your home, you may be able to get a third mortgage. By using the equity in your home as collateral, you stand to benefit because you will normally be entitled to apply the interest on the loan to your income-tax deductions just as you would with your first mortgage. Ask your accountant or tax attorney about the best way to approach the potential tax benefits.

The questions remain: Where can you find a lender, and will you qualify for the loan? There are several places to look for loans. Often, contractors themselves will have information on available lenders. The remodeler may do business with several banks as a result of customers who have used them for financing. Some lenders solicit contractors as middlemen to help sell their financing services. Some lenders advertise through contractor publications or at trade shows. It certainly does not hurt to ask candidates for your remodeling job if they know of lenders who finance home improvement projects.

Another source for such loans referrals is a real estate agent. Banks often solicit the help of brokers in getting the word out to homeowners. They try to publicize their home purchase loans through real estate agencies. These banks are good places to look for loans. Call a real estate agent and ask for a list of lenders. Even if you have not done business with a real estate agent in a while, you should not feel shy about asking for this favor. Brokers are usually happy to establish acquaintances with local homeowners. It's good business because you represent a potential sale and commission to them when you want to buy or sell somewhere down the line.

Home purchasers frequently go to loan brokers to find loans. These are professionals who are paid commissions by banks for bringing customers to them. Often, the cost of this commission is passed on to the borrower in the form of slightly higher interest rates or larger "points." "Points" means the up-front lending fee that the lender charges for the loan in addition to interest charges. A point equals 1 percent (a percentage point). A $10,000 loan with a 2-point fee means that the lender will charge $200 in points for the loan. When you borrow through a broker, up to 1 additional point may be added onto the loan, although it would not be quoted to you that way. The broker will simply tell you that there are 2.5 or 3 points on the loan—instead of the normal 2 points otherwise charged with a nonbrokered loan.

But this is not necessarily the case. Brokers and lenders must compete. And because brokers represent many banks, they may be able to get you a good deal if you bargain hard. Treat loan brokers as you would treat car dealers. Bargain hard and don't trust them. Play one off against another and compare what loan deals a broker offers with what the banks will get you. Lie if you have to. You never know how far a branch will bend until you try. (Just don't break the broker.) Again, if you need to, study up on The Rule of the Psychological Hump in the Introduction before you confront a broker.

And you can always find banks listed in the yellow pages. Call around. Find out what kind of deals are available. Duration of the loan, interest rates, low rates with a balloon payment versus higher payments that pay off the principal over the life of the loan, points, application fees and miscellaneous charges—all should be considered in choosing a lender and a loan. A bank may keep these costs down or eliminate them altogether during a special promotion, and this break may more than compensate for a slightly higher interest rate.

The Federal Housing Administration (FHA) has a program by which it insures loans for home improvements through participating banks. The FHA guarantees to the bank that the loan will be repaid. The FHA requires that the lender individually approve any contractor arranging for an FHA loan. But neither the bank nor the FHA guarantees the work. Contractors' saying that they are FHA-approved is meaningless. So beware of those who make such assertions; they may mean only that the contractors were approved for FHA-funded projects in the past. They do not necessarily mean that the tasks were performed with any degree of competence.

If you are finding it hard to get a bank loan, look for the Federal Housing Authority, Federal Housing Administration, or Department of Housing and Urban Development in the federal government listings (blue pages) in your telephone directory. They should be able to direct you to someone who can help you find a bank that has FHA-insured funds.

My Favorite: The "Mutually Beneficial Family Loan"

Many people hate to tuck their tails between their legs and ask their parents, siblings, uncles, cousins, or friends to help them out with a loan. But what if you would be doing *them* a favor by borrowing the money? First, you must find a relative who has cash available. Maybe it's languishing in a savings account. Or perhaps a certificate of deposit (CD) is about to mature.

Here is how what I call the Mutually Beneficial Family Loan (MBFL) works. Your relative—or friend—has money in the bank or in a CD or other investment, such as bonds, that is earning 6 percent interest. The banks are offering home improvement loans at 10 percent. If you could get the loan from your relative at 8 percent interest, you would be saving 2 percent per year in addition to avoiding points, the application fee, appraisal fee, document fees, and the like. Your lending relative's money will be earning two full percentage points more than it would in a bank.

You protect the relative's interest by writing out a loan agreement. You can either obtain blank forms at an office-supply store or write your own.

Your local bank should be able to furnish you with a booklet of monthly payment tables. Look up the page for the proposed interest rate in the book and then go down the column to locate the amount of the loan. Look across the table for the duration of the loan. The table will show you how much the monthly payments should be for a fully amortized loan (a loan by which the interest and principal are both paid off in monthly installment payments). You may want to consult your accountant for more information.

If you wish to simply pay interest on the loan for a period of years and then pay off the principal at the end of that period (a balloon payment), simply take the annual interest rate—let's say 9 percent—and divide it by twelve monthly payments. That means 0.75% per month. On a $20,000 loan, it would work like this:

0.09 (9 percent interest) ÷ 12 (months) = .0075
     (1 month's 0.75 percent interest)
0.0075 (1 month interest) × $20,000 = $150 (each month's interest)

Therefore, $150 will be due on the loan each month until the balance of $20,000 is due in a balloon payment.

You might want to ask your bank whether it provides joint control services or whether it can recommend a joint control—or funding control—company. This will simplify the control of your home improvement project and will get the bank involved in seeing to it that funds are not squandered (see Chapters 3 and 5).

The Tax Bonus

If you register the loan with your local government tax agency, you will establish it as a true mortgage loan, so long as the loan agreement states that the house itself is collateral for the loan. If you already have a mortgage on the house (a first trust deed), this will be your second trust deed. If you already have a second trust deed on the property, this will be a third trust deed, and so on. When you register the trust deed with the tax agency, it means that the mortgage holder—the person who loaned you the money—must have his or her remaining principal paid off upon the sale of the home, if it hasn't been already. The relative has a partial ownership in the home and therefore has the right of approval on any transaction that would transfer ownership of the property.

I must warn you that you should check these procedures with an attorney, an accountant, or the Internal Revenue Service (IRS). You must be sure that the IRS will recognize the loan as a legitimate mortgage. This will preclude any possibility of the tax deduction's being disallowed after you file your return.

Keep in mind that the lender will have to report any interest income from the loan on his or her return. However, this is no different from the requirement to report income from most other investments.

A Scenario

Arleen and Jerry have a kitchen that has not been remodeled since the house was built in 1927. (That was the year in which Babe Ruth hit sixty homers and Charles A. Lindbergh soloed across the Atlantic.) They have been saving money for a renovation but so far have accumulated only about five grand. What to do? A light bulb goes on in Jerry's cranium. "Why don't we borrow from your parents?" he asks Arleen. "After all, they're always asking us if we need anything. I don't want their money. But what if we could borrow from them in a way that's profitable for them as well as for us?"

Because Arleen has a close relationship with her parents, she feels comfortable going to them for help. And because they care so much for her and for Jerry, it isn't difficult for them to talk about finances. So off they go to Arleen's parents. Jerry makes the pitch: "Mom, Dad (he calls them that when he's after something), Arleen and I have a proposition to make. We need to refurbish our kitchen. We figure that it will cost us about $20,000. We've set aside about $5,000 for just that purpose. But it will take us about another four years to save the rest. We're desperate for a new fridge and a new dishwasher, and since the baby was born we need a new washer and dryer. And we've run out of storage space. So we were wondering if you would lend us the $15,000."

"That's a lot of money, darling," responds Arleen's mother. "Dad and I have the money in a CD and count on it for our own income."

Arleen asks, "If you don't mind my asking, how much is the CD paying?"

"It's okay," replies Dad. "It pays 6½ percent. But if we loaned you the money, we couldn't possibly let you pay us interest."

"But why not?" is Jerry's query. "The bank pays you 4 percent less than it would charge us for a home improvement loan. We could pay you 8½ percent and still save 2 percent under what they would charge us. Plus Arleen and I will save on points, application fees, the appraisal cost, and the like. We'll give you a second mortgage on the property in case we both should die, and we'll save on our income taxes. Everybody will benefit except the banks."

Arleen's parents look at each other, smile and Dad says, "Kids, we love you both. You are smart and practical and you make a hell of a case for yourselves. Of course we'll lend you the money. How could we resist such a deal?"

Is this a fairy tale? Absolutely. Could it work? Absolutely. You just need the right people who are willing to make the loan. They don't even have to trust you—but it helps.

Insurance Policies

Insurance companies offer more types of life insurance and retirement policies than you can shake a stick at. (Yeah, like anyone can have more of *anything* than you could shake a stick at—but I digress.) Many of these policies offer you the option of borrowing against the funds that you've contributed to your insurance. This is a complicated subject to deal with because a lot depends on the type of policy you are borrowing against. Get your broker, accountant, or tax attorney to advise you about this option. Retirement policies are loaded with tax-deduction complexities.

Things to Remember

1. There are several sources for the financing of home improvement projects. They include banks, independent lending institutions, family, and friends.

2. Borrowing against the equity in your home gives you the advantage of an income-tax deduction.

3. Your broker may be able to refer you to a lender who specializes in home improvement loans.

4. Real estate brokers may have available lists of lenders.

5. Brokers can also find you loans, but sometimes you will have to pay a slightly higher rate or loan fee.

6. You can find lenders in newspapers or the yellow pages.

7. You can look for an FHA-approved loan through the Department of Housing and Urban Development.

8. If you have a compliant relative or friend, you can arrange what I call the Mutually Beneficial Family Loan (MBFL). It will save you money and earn money for the lender.

9. If you properly register the MBFL, you will retain the tax benefits of a home mortgage.

10. Consider borrowing against your life insurance.

5

Getting the Job Done

"I'm really upset that the plumbing hasn't been installed yet," said the homeowner.

"I'm the contractor. Let me worry about it. It'll get done," responded the contractor. "By the way, isn't your next payment due?"

"I'm a banker," answered the homeowner, "Let me worry about it. It'll get paid."

The Attitude

Conflict is the last thing you want during the course of your home remodeling project. Well, not necessarily the *last* thing—but it ranks right up there with things going wrong, late completion, noncompletion, and sloppy work. What it has in common with all of the other problems is that the other problems often will lead to conflict. It is very important that you give contractors the benefit of the doubt in this sense: Assume that they are trying to do their best; that they are being sincere in their efforts to get the job done properly. This leads to a more harmonious style of communication. Save belligerence for when things are screwed up and the contractor is indifferent to your plight.

This does not mean that you should put your suspicions about the contractor aside or that you should ignore blatantly defective work or a cavalier attitude. Be cautious, but don't act outwardly suspicious. If you have cold water coming out of the hot-water faucet on your new bathroom sink—and vice versa—you don't have to put up with contractors who say, "You'll get used to it." You are entitled to get what you have agreed to and what you are paying for. But keep up a good relationship if you can. Try to see the situation from the contractor's side. But don't compromise what you feel you have a right to expect. Let the contractors *prove* to you that they've screwed up.

Only by taking a conciliatory approach in your relationship with the contractors can you ride out the bumps of the remodeling process. (Sounds sort of like marriage.) Welcome the workers and the contractor to your home. Offer them something to quench their thirsts from time to time. Ask about their personal lives. Let them know a little about you. In other words, set up the situation so that you can become human beings to one another. In this way, when you have to hash things out during unexpected crises, you will already have made every effort to establish a compatible relationship. (Sounds even more like marriage.) There should be no question that you have given the benefit of the doubt to the contracor when a seemingly unresolvable dispute arises. Then you will know that when you-know-what hits the fan, you have tried everything to be reasonable.

The day that you hand over the down payment, or deposit, to the contractor is when this attitude should start. When work starts, welcome him and his crew to your property. Don't give them the run of the place or the combination to your safe. Just be friendly.

Finances

For a large remodeling job, it is advisable to set up a separate checking or savings account unless you are using joint funding. If you use a savings account, make sure that you still make all payments by money order or check so that you have irrefutable proof of payment.

The reason for setting up a separate account is that you want to be able to see how you are disbursing your funds. Also, you don't want to intermingle the money you have set aside or borrowed for the project with other household funds. With a separate account you can keep clear records of what you are spending.

If you borrow from a bank or other lending institution in the form of a home equity loan and the bank is not furnishing funding control, the funds will usually be made available in the form of a checking account. This is the perfect device for disbursing funds and keeping records. Otherwise, simply open a new account and place the funds for the project into it.

The Job Begins

The first few days are usually the noisiest, dustiest, and most upsetting. Often a demolition crew comes in and rips out the old . . . (fill in this space yourself—choices include but are not limited to plumbing fixtures, tiles, walls, roof, flooring, light fixtures, kitchen cabinets, doors, windows, and rain gutters). The house shakes, the banging gives you the feeling that your home is being murdered, and you're sure that the building will collapse. With any luck, the kids will be at school, and you and your spouse will be at work, so at least you won't have to witness the carnage.

If you are adding a floor and part of your ceiling is being mauled while there are workers up above who are literally stripping away the roof over your head, the experience can be terrifying. My family doctor recently decided to have a second story added onto his house when he and his wife learned that they were expecting their third child. But since they decided that they would not want to endure the ensuing torture, they decided to rent another house for a few months while their own domicile underwent a facelift. But he could afford to do that—he's a doctor.

During the first couple of days you can set the tone for your working relationship with the contractor, who should be there in person to see that work begins smoothly and in the manner agreed to. A crew should not show up to start demolition, alteration, or construction without the contractor's being there to give instructions on exactly what is expected of them.

At the end of the day the work site, and especially the parts of your home adjacent to the work area, should be relatively tidy. If you do not receive this type of service, it is time for you to let the contractor know that you are not satisfied. Be diplomatic, friendly, but firm. On the other hand, if things go swimmingly, give him a verbal pat on the back and reinforce his operating methods. A contractor who likes you is apt to be more diligent about pleasing you.

Protecting Yourself from Mechanics' Liens

Suppliers' Liens

Soon after (or even before) work begins, the materials will be brought to your home. If your contract provides that your first postdeposit payment will be due at this point, it is time for the contractor to provide you with lien releases for all materials that have been delivered. Since you have already paid a deposit, the contractor should have used the funds for the purchase of materials. If he brings up the fact that according to your contract, lien releases are to apply only up to the time of the previous payment, he will be right. Concede the point graciously. So why bother? You have just let the contractor know that you are on top of things.

Here is where careful record keeping becomes important. Each time materials are brought to your home, it is imperative that you determine who the suppliers are. If you see the supplier's truck arrive, ask how much of which materials are being delivered. And don't sign for any deliveries. Materials should be delivered to the general contractor—not to the owner. If you sign for deliveries, you could be held accountable for them. Unless it was agreed that you would be supplying certain materials, like appliances, for the project, do not get involved in doing what should be the contractor's job.

Get a copy of the invoice and write down the information in some sort of binder. Why is this important? I'm glad I asked. Allow me to answer by way of an example.

A homeowner sees a stack of lumber that he rightfully assumes was delivered to his property because it was ordered by the contractor. The next day, the homeowner returns home from work and notices that a substantial portion of the lumber is no longer in the stack. He assumes that the carpenters are working really fast and that the lumber has been used on the job. Right? Wrong! During the day, the contractor picked up the now-missing lumber and moved it over to another job she is working on. According to the supplier's records the lumber was for our friend's project. The supplier knows nothing of the other job. In fact, this particular contractor does this type of thing all the time. She simply moves deliveries to other job sites and depends on her customers' not being careful about their payments.

But, you retort, since I have a contract that limits the amount I will have to pay the contractor, what do I have to worry about? The odds are that you are right. But what if you are one of those unfortunate people who hire a remodeler just before he goes under? If he skips town without all his bills paid but with a lot of cash collected from unfinished jobs, you could get stuck owing payments to lumberyards, appliance suppliers, lighting wholesalers, window distributors, and who knows who else. If the material was delivered to your property, you could find yourself at the wrong end of a mechanic's lien.

There have been cases in which shady remodelers have ordered supplies for two or more jobs to be delivered to one work site. The supplier assumes that the project at that site is the one that will be using the materials. The contractor then takes some of the supplies over to another work site or two, and the entire cost of the shipment goes on the supplier's records for the location to which the load was delivered. The contractor then hides the source of the delivery from the customer by never showing the customer the invoice from that supplier. Following is an illustration.

Don and Gloria are adding on to their house. The first lumber delivery came from Jesse's Lumberyard. The contractor showed Don the invoice and later showed him a lien release from Jesse. Then another shipment of lumber came. But it was from Julie's Building Supply. The delivery was made when neither Gloria nor Don was at home. The contractor loaded half of the lumber onto his truck and carted it away to another job he was working on. Don and Gloria never knew about it. They had no reason to suspect that there was a second lumber supplier, so they never asked for a lien waiver. After the job was finished and the contractor was paid, Don and Gloria received a notice from Julie's Building Supply that they owed $2,000 for materials delivered to their home. And in most states they would be liable for it unless they could get the contractor to pay up. If he hasn't skipped town it is likely that since he was such a s.o.b. to begin with he might put them through the wringer before he pays up. And who wants to go through all of that hassle?

What was their mistake? Gloria and Don should have noticed the new supply of lumber on their property after the second delivery (the one from Julie's Building Supply). At that point they should have insisted on seeing the invoice for it, recorded the delivery information from the invoice, and seen to it that the lien releases matched the invoices.

Okay, you say, let's get real here. Who has the time, energy, or inclination to go through all this checking, rechecking, and record keeping? The truth is, if you meticulously followed all the instructions for choosing a contractor in Chapter 2 and you were diligent in making a contract as instructed in Chapter 3, you should be feeling pretty good about your dealings with the contractor at this point. I know that when Cheryl and I had a kitchen remodeling job done we felt so good about our contractor that we were not as diligent as we might have been. And everything turned out better than expected. The more complex and costly the project, the more chances for skullduggery and honest mistakes.

You have to use your best judgment. However, careful record keeping cannot hurt unless you have a cranky contractor. But if you let contractors know that you want everything to run in a businesslike manner, they should be willing to make the effort to please you. Personalities play a big part in the relationship between owners and contractors. If you show them respect and that you understand their reluctance to go through the extra trouble of showing you invoices and accounting for every delivery, they should respect your diligence and concern about the quality of the work being done. If not, you may have chosen the wrong contractor. Which is even more of a reason to want to keep tabs on him.

Subcontractor Liens

When a worker or crew shows up at your property they will either be employees of the contractor or they will be employees of one of his or her subcontractors. For the same reasons that apply to suppliers, you should determine for whom these people work. If a subcontractor does work on your property and you are not aware of it, you will have no way of knowing that you need a mechanic's lien waiver from that particular sub. Again, you could be in jeopardy if the sub is not properly paid by the contractor.

As an additional precaution, you could ask the contractor for the name of each subcontracting company he has working on the site on a daily basis.

Note, if you are using a joint control (or funding control) company, that these firms do perform inspections, but *only* to see what stage of completion the work is at. This is done just so they can determine if scheduled payments should be made. Normally, they *do not* inspect for quality or specification compliance.

If you hired an architect to design the job, you should have included in your contract with her that she will inspect the remodeling project on a regular basis for quality and specification compliance.

Record Keeping

From the foregoing discussion, you can see why record keeping is so important. Using an accordion folder and your checkbook or ledger will make record keeping simple. Use the folder sections to hold your invoices, notations of delivery, and a list of subcontractors, grouped by payment periods as determined by your contract schedule. Each time there is a payment due, you will know which lien releases should be forthcoming before you make payment.

Change Orders

When unforeseen problems arise during the course of the job, or when you change your mind about what you want done, you must change the terms of your contract. Specifications as to materials, design, added or lowered expenses, methodology, schedule changes, and the like must be agreed to in writing according to the terms of the contract. It is essential that, once again, *everything be in writing*—and signed and dated by all parties concerned.

When Cheryl and I were having our duplex rental unit kitchen remodeled, the plumbing subcontractors opened the wall behind the sink and found that the drainpipe in the wall was corroded and had not been installed properly according to today's standards. Our contractor informed us that he could leave it as is—with the likelihood that it would either back up or start leaking sooner or later—or the plumbers could make it conform to current building codes. By this time the contractor had earned our trust through his business manner. The additional cost would be $300. We went for it. Because it was not going to add time to the completion deadline and the amount of money was small, we did not execute a change order.

In theory, that was a mistake. In fact, everything went smoothly. But what if the job had taken a week longer to complete? Or what if the drain had stopped up a month later, the contractor had refused to fix it, and I couldn't prove that he had upgraded it? Or what if the final bill came in for an extra million dollars? Okay, I'm getting carried away. But you get the point.

Here are some common reasons for change orders: You decide that carpeting won't go with the paint. You want a skylight added. You see a room on a TV show that knocks your socks off, so you want to copy some of the windows, doors, and arches. Your father-in-law comes to visit and says, "You're not going to put dark mahogany flooring in a room that only gets northern light. You need a nice light-colored wood. It'll make the room look bigger." (Besides, you shouldn't be using tropical wood anyway. It means destroying tropical trees, and that depletes the rainforests and hastens the destruction of our atmosphere.)

Or you decide that you are overspending and that you have to cut back on some of your indulgences in order to keep from borrowing on your credit cards. So you go for ordinary tiles in the bath and kitchen, you opt for chrome plumbing fixtures instead of brass, and you decide on prefab instead of custom-made kitchen cabinets.

Your contractor should have a supply of change order forms. More large jobs involve change orders than don't. But keep in mind that a change order is itself a contract. It involves a renegotiation. Understand everything in it, including the fine print. If the contractor says that the fine print means stuff other than what it seems to mean, write out the explanation on the contract and have the contractor initial the explanation. Draw lines through any unused blanks. And keep a copy.

And where does the copy go? Right. In the file. Along with the contract. To simplify things for yourself, you may want to extract the essentials of the change order and put them on a separate sheet that you can refer to conveniently without having to wade through any more complicated changes.

Written and Telephone Communications

You will want to keep a record of all essential communications. Sometimes a brief exchange takes place between the homeowner and the contractor that is not worthy of a change order. Suppose that after you have the tile installed in your bathroom you decide that Benjamin Moore's canary yellow is not the right color paint for the walls. You would rather have lemon à la mode paint. So you call the contractor, who acknowledges the change. At this point you should send a dated note to that effect and ask the contractor either to sign the note and return it to you (enclosing a self-addressed, stamped envelope will make compliance more likely) or to send you a dated, signed confirming note. File the note in your accordion file. If the painters start slapping canary yellow on the walls, you will have simple proof that you and the contractor agreed to a change.

It's also a good idea to make notations about any telephone conversations between you and the remodeler. Just in case your note isn't returned, or if something significant was mentioned, it is a good idea to have a "hard" record of it in case a dispute arises later.

Supervising the Job

Imagine, if you will, that you walk into your kitchen during the renovation project to see what it looks like with new cabinets and you find that the upper cupboards—all twelve sections of them—extend all the way up to the ceiling. They look fine, but the contract calls for cabinets that are wall-mounted and are twenty-seven inches high, and the installed cabinets are thirty-six inches high. The reason for the shorter cabinets was that you wanted to exhibit your pottery collection on top of them, and also you don't want to store bread crumbs in the top of a cupboard you'd have to stand on a stool to reach.

You call the contractor to tell him and he's ticked off. He says, "Why didn't you say something two days ago when they installed the first two cupboards?" How did this happen? First, the contractor goofed by purchasing the wrong cabinets. Second, you goofed by not supervising the job on a daily—or near-daily—basis. Best of all would be if you or your spouse took a gander at the deliveries and the work on a daily basis.

If things get out of hand, you may be technically in the right, but think of how the contractor would feel about the prospect of ripping out the new cabinets, returning them to the supplier, purchasing replacements, and reinstalling them. If you hold the contractor to the contract you can be fairly sure that he will not be inclined to do you any favors.

You have the right to supervise and inspect if you executed your contract as suggested in Chapter 3. Exercise this right. You may feel uncomfortable telling other people how to do their jobs. That's understandable. But you have to deal only with the general contractor. You should not give instructions directly to subs, workers, or suppliers. That is the contractor's job. Don't get caught in the middle. And it is easier to confront uncomfortable situations by asking questions. "I noticed that the painters are painting in the new bedroom. We are supposed to have wallpaper in there. Are they doing the right thing?" is a better way of approaching the issue than saying, "Get over here right away. Those jokers are painting where they should be wallpapering!" It could be that the wall is being primed first before the paper goes on. It is better for the contractor to answer a question than to give you information in a way that embarrasses you and puts him in an adversarial position.

On the other hand, if you notice that the window installers are about to install bay windows in a place where a picture window belongs, it would be appropriate for you to tell them to stop while you get the contractor on the phone and ask, "Why are the installers putting bay windows in the north wall of the den?" A short delay would be a lot better than having your new wall mutilated when the wrong windows are extricated.

Architects and Engineers

If you are having new structural members (beams, roof trusses, or the like) added to your property, major plumbing additions done, ductwork added, central air-conditioning installed, new roofing put on, or any other major changes or additions, it is advisable that you hire a professional to inspect the work. If you hired an architect to design the home improvement, see to it that the contract with the architect includes his or her performing on-site inspections on a regular basis. The architect's wisdom may be worth a fortune to you, to say nothing of the delays, frustration, inconvenience, and downright desire to commit homicide that it could save you.

Installation of mechanical systems should be inspected and approved by engineers who specialize in the respective fields. You don't want to watch water dripping through your new ceiling because the condensation on your air-conditioning ducts is dripping inside the ceiling and through the new plaster onto your expensive hardwood flooring. The subcontractor, upon whom the general contractor relied, may have made an understandable mistake, but that understanding won't be enough to calm you down when the flooring and the ceiling have to be ripped open. Your architect, funding control company, and lender are sources of engineers. Do not use an engineer who is associated with the contractor or sub for the inspection. There would be a conflict of interest.

During more costly renovations, it is in the lender's interest to want inspectors at the work site as money is being disbursed. Lenders don't want their funds sunk into a project that will have to be torn down because someone overlooked a structural necessity.

Building Inspectors

Building improvements in virtually every locality are controlled to some extent by government regulatory agencies. Water supply, waste disposal, construction, use zoning, proximity to other structures, hazard potential, and any number of other variables must meet with the approval of agencies responsible for the protection of all parties affected by the improvements, as well as protection of the natural environment. As the work on your property progresses, it will have to undergo repeated inspections. Before any phase of construction can be completed, it must receive an "okay" from a building inspector, water department inspector, environmental agency inspector, concrete inspector, or one of any number of other inspectors, depending on the job and upon where you are having the work done. To contractors, this is usually a pain in a part of the anatomy where the sun don't shine. Keep this in mind: Delays due to inspection problems are the concern of the contractor. They are not your problem. Inspectors, believe it or not, are there to protect *you*. They are there to see that the improvements on your home don't harm or kill you or members of your family. They have nothing to gain by determining that the work is not sufficient to pass inspection (unless they're crooks— and we all know that there are none of those in government). They have no motives—unless they hate your contractor—to arbitrarily fail the work.

So how are inspectors your friends? (I ask great questions, don't I?) They protect you from shoddy work in those areas of construction or improvements that are most vital. If the remodeler ever says to you, "I think I can do this phase of the job without the city ever knowing about it. We can save money on the building permits and save time by not waiting for inspections," it is in your interest to insist that you want the work done "by the book." Getting away without inspections means that the contractors' work might get away with being second-rate. Don't be penny wise and dollar foolish. Faulty wiring, insufficient structural supports, and insufficient plumbing could prove to be nuisances, if not fatal flaws, in a few months.

As a matter of fact, anytime that you can be present for a government inspection, do so. You can learn from the inspector what the contractor is handling well and where the weaknesses, if any, are. It gives you the opportunity to open a discussion with the contractor about the way he's handling things—positive or negative. You can also pick the inspectors' brains—there's a pretty picture—about how he feels the work is going. If you are looking for an inspection engineer for upcoming work, the government inspector might be able to put you on the right track.

Finally, make sure that you keep tabs on inspections. There is a form, often a card displayed by the contractor at the job site, that shows the progress of inspections. Know what is going on, and don't hesitate to ask questions.

Doing Your Own Inspections

In addition to supervising and inspecting the job within the limitations described in Chapter 3, you should also be checking less obvious contingencies. My brother-in-law lives in what is called a bachelor apartment. It has an unusual entrance. The door is pushed open from the corridor side; upon entering the foyer, one sees a wall directly ahead and must make an immediate sharp turn to the left in order to enter the main room. This would not be significant except that no large furniture can be brought into the apartment because of the narrow entrance clearance. Neither can a full-size stove or a regular refrigerator.

I once saw a story on television about a contractor who, although he met substantial-completion requirements, was being sued by a homeowner because, among other things, the family-room addition that was built was three inches shorter than the plans called for. This may seem like a petty gripe, but not when you consider that the room dimensions were determined by the furniture that was going into the room. The family had an expensive sofa and bookcase that were to fit along one wall. The sofa would not fit because of the three-inch misjudgment.

You might help prevent these types of mistakes by going through the work site periodically and checking it out. Does the door opening look right? Are the necessary measurements correct? Does any part of the design—which looked great on paper when you and the contractor or architect agreed upon it—bring doubts to your mind today? This is the time for your questions and doubts to be raised. It would be terrible for you to suppress those doubts until the job is completed and it's time to hand over the final check.

Making Payments

Your contract provides that payments will be made according to schedule. If you remember from Chapter 3, these payments are an important way for you to protect yourself from those few unscrupulous general contractors who don't pay their stubs and suppliers but pocket the money instead and force you into dealing with mechanics' liens.

According to your contract, payments should be made by completion of phases of the remodeling job—not by dates. If you are taking care of the payments directly, you must stick to your guns. If the contractor, suppliers, and subs are being paid through a funding control (joint control) company, you have less to worry about because the company is being paid to stay on top of these things.

If the contractor says to you, "I know that the kitchen cabinets haven't been installed yet, but I need the money to pay my people and keep them on the job," you must respond by saying something like, "I'm sorry, but we signed the contract together. This is a business arrangement, and it's my only way of protecting myself." If the contract calls for the third payment upon installation of the kitchen cabinets, that's when you hand over the check.

Do not pay for goods and services not yet received. And never pay until you receive the lien releases from all subs, all suppliers, and the general contractor. Remember, the lien releases should cover all materials and labor up until the date of the most recent previous payment.

Earlier in this chapter I explained about keeping track of all work crews and deliveries. If you don't remember, go back and peruse it now. I'll wait. Here's why it's important.

A general contractor can present you with all kinds of releases from subs and suppliers. But unless you have releases from *all* the subs and suppliers, you may never know whether you will be hit by a lien notice from someone you've never heard of. If the first delivery of lumber came from a particular lumberyard and you duly noted the source of the delivery and the quantity of the lumber, but the next lumber delivery is from another vendor and you weren't around for the delivery, you could be in trouble. That delivery might never be paid for. And your assumption that the first lumber supplier is the only lumber supplier can work against you.

The remodeler can present you with evidence that all suppliers have been paid at the time he collects payment from you. But if he knows that you are unaware of the existence of one of his suppliers, he can hide the information from you, never present you with a lien release, and then get away without paying for a delivery from that supplier.

Similar situations can arise if a contractor uses several carpenters, floor layers, painting subs, and . . . well, you get the idea. So it is a good idea to try to keep track of everyone who delivers to—or works on—your job site. If you can't check up on it, maybe your spouse or friend or someone else you trust can.

If, however, you and everyone you know has a life and can't hang around keeping an eye on things, try this. When you get home, look over what work has been done and what has been delivered. Then call the contractor and ask who delivered to, or worked on, the property. The next day, call the supplier or the subcontractor and ask whether they delivered, installed, built, or serviced at your property the day before. If they didn't, you have to determine where the goods or services came from. You must tell the contractor that you called the supplier or sub and that they did not confirm the delivery or service. Before you lose your temper, though, keep in mind that there may be extenuating circumstances that make the contractor blameless.

It could be that the contractor merely confused who made the repair or delivered the goods to your site. If he or she is dealing with several jobs at a time, it could be easy to confuse them. It is also possible that the sub or the supplier confused your project with another one.

Just be sure that you straighten out any misunderstanding before you have an argument. It's a lot like marriage. At the risk of repeating myself, it boils down to this: As you make each payment, be sure that you know exactly which materials and what labor you are paying for. Confirm that you know the true source of each labor job and each material supply. Get the appropriate mechanics' lien releases before you hand the check over to the remodeler. Your contract calls for certain work to have been completed before each payment. Make sure that the contractor's obligation has been met. Do not make payment based on his promise.

What else can you do to make sure that general contractors are not getting away without paying their subs and suppliers? Be sure that you have included in your contract a stipulation which says that final payment on your project will not be due until a sufficient time after the job is completed in order to allow lien claimants to notify you. Allow me to clarify. In California, mechanics' liens must be declared within thirty days of job completion. A sub or supplier who wants to put a lien upon your property must notify you of that fact within thirty days after you agree with the general contractor that the job is finished. A sub or supplier who waits beyond that time loses the right to file for a lien against you and must go after the remodeler. Only after the thirty days expires should you pay the final amount to the remodeler. This is the one way in which you can be absolutely sure that you will not be defending yourself in court against an angry lien claimant.

You must determine from your state regulatory agency (see Appendix A) what the lien claim period limitation is. If you are using funding control, the joint control company will usually insist on this procedure. I advise you to make sure when you first commence business with joint control that it does so. In California, this principle is called retention. It means that the contract between the funding control company and the contractor states that the final 10 percent (or 5 percent or anything in between) will be retained until thirty days after completion of the project.

In order to properly establish completion of the project, file a notice of completion at your county recorder's office. Never allow the contractor to do it for you. Forms may be obtained from stores that sell preprinted forms or from title companies or lenders. If you have financed your home improvement project through a lending institution, the lender may insist upon filing—in which case you should request a copy.

Once you have recorded your notice of completion, the clock starts ticking for the subs and suppliers to file their lien notices, if any.

You will also want to have the originals of all warranties, guarantees, and instruction manuals that come with any of the products the contractor installed, such as roofing materials, fixtures, appliances, water heaters, and the like.

You will also need all permits that were obtained from government agencies as well as records of inspection signed off by the inspectors. And don't forget the final list of all suppliers and subs.

If your contract does not specify all of these requirements for final payment, it should. Nay, it must.

Additional Improvements

What should you do in the event the contractor comes to you with an idea that sounds great but will cost you additional bucks?

Arleen and Jerry were happy with the way their second-story addition was progressing when the contractor approached them with an idea. "I could," he proposed, "eliminate one of the bedroom windows and add a sliding patio door. Outside, I can build a deck that would extend along the side of the house. I can then install a door in the hallway that also gives access to the deck. This way your family and guests can get to the deck without going through your bedroom."

"How much?" asked Jerry as suspiciously as possible.

"Five thousand. And the overhang of the deck would create a patio below."

"Excuse us," Arleen responded, yanking Jerry into the next room. They discussed the pros and cons of the proposal.

"It sounds nice and would add to the value of the house, but I don't know if it's worth it," Jerry said.

"We could try bargaining with him," responded Arleen.

"Yeah, we could. But we have no way to get competitors' bids. So we don't know what it's worth."

"I wonder if he's just trying to get an unreasonable amount of money out of us," wondered Arleen.

"Hey, I've got it. Let's call the architect. He could give us an idea as to what the job should cost."

"Yeah. And we can ask the joint control company what they think. Maybe one of their people could give us an idea."

"Right," said Jerry. "And your parents added on a deck a few years ago. Let's find out what it cost them. Then we could find out what a reasonable price for a regular door and a patio door would be. We could price them at the building-supply place and then try to estimate what the installation would cost."

"Great," affirmed Arleen. "And in a pinch we could always pay a specialty contractor to act as a consultant. He could give us an honest estimate if he knew that we would not be hiring him for the job."

"Yeah, yeah. That's the ticket. Now let's decide how high we would be willing to go if we decided to do this."

You get the idea. You don't want to be taken advantage of by a contractor who knows that you are not going to seek competing bids in the middle of a project. So you need to decide if the new idea is a *good* idea. Is it worth the cost? Then use your resources to investigate its worthiness. The example of Arleen and Jerry is simply an illustration. And it may not be applicable if you "follow your guts" (see Chapter 2) and you have faith in your contractor.

Don't forget to allow a little extra for the remodeler's time and effort. And, as always, don't forget the change orders, the allowance for extra completion time, and the additional inconveniences.

Things to Remember

1. As much as possible, maintain a friendly disposition from the first encounter to the final payment. Take the attitude that you're working on the project *together*, not as adversaries. Save anger for the time when all else fails, *if* that should unfortunately happen.

2. If a dispute arises, try to see things from the contractor's point of view before coming to a final conclusion.

3. Be friendly and welcoming to workers. It predisposes them to do a good job for you.

4. If you are making the payments to the contractor yourself, keep a separate bank account in order to control expenses closely.

5. Expect chaos the first few days, especially if demolition work is done.

6. Whenever a work crew arrives for the first time, the remodeler should be there to acquaint them with the job.

7. You are entitled to a relatively clean work site at the end of each workday, if so stated in your contract.

8. Along the way, don't forget to give the workers and the general contractor a pat on the back for work well done.

9. If possible, keep track of all deliveries made to your work site. Check to see that the invoice matches the materials, and hold onto a copy.

10. Don't sign for deliveries unless by written agreement with the contractor. It is the contractor's responsibility to accept deliveries. If the contractor picks up the material and delivers it to the site, make sure that you compare the delivered material with what is listed on his invoice or receipt from the supplier.

11. When workers first show up at your property, determine whom they are employed by and keep track of when, and on what, they worked.

12. If you hired an architect to design the job, you should have included in your contract that the architect will inspect the remodeling project on a regular basis for quality and specification compliance.

13. Keep complete files of your project, including correspondence, dated notations of conversations, payments, change orders, deliveries, and notations of work done.

14. When *any* changes from the original contract are agreed upon, they must be recorded on a printed *change order*.

15. Supervise the job by looking at the work on a daily basis and seeing whether it complies with the contract.

16. Consider the use of engineers to inspect the installation of complex systems such as air-conditioning, plumbing, and septic tanks.

17. Government building inspectors are a good source of feedback as to the sufficiency of some of the vital work being done. Get as much information from them as you can.

18. If the remodeler complains that a government inspector is being unreasonable, it is a sign that you need to get direct input from that inspector.

19. Keep a record of all government inspections.

20. Do your own inspections to see that the work is done according to contract specifications. This could help you catch any variances in the work before they get out of hand.

21. Make payments only as the required phases of completion are reached—not by dates. Do not vary from this procedure. Never pay for materials or services that you haven't yet received.

22. Make no payments until you have lien releases from *all* subs and suppliers for goods and services provided through the date of the previous scheduled payment.

23. At the end of a workday when no one from your household is around to keep an eye on things, determine which subs or suppliers provided goods and services. Make sure that all of these people supply lien releases for subsequent payments.

24. Confirm all alleged deliveries or services with the actual suppliers and subcontractors. If there is a discrepancy, make sure that the contractor corrects or explains it.

25. The person who is filing a mechanic's lien must notify the property owner within a set limit of time. Make sure that you do not make final payment to the general contractor until that time period has passed since completion of the job.

26. File a notice of completion at the county recorder's office as soon as work is completed. But do not make final payment until you have received all appropriate documentation.

27. If the remodeler comes up with an idea that sounds good but that will cost you substantially more money, weigh it carefully. Consult your architect, joint control, suppliers, or specialty contractors to determine if the improvement is worth the money.

28. Remember that such changes could affect not only cost but also additional time, inconvenience, and, possibly, new financial arrangements with your lender. Be sure that all such changes are agreed to in writing on change orders.

6

Correcting Mistakes and Resolving Disputes

The judge looked at the contractor and said, "You claim that the defendant owes you $5,000 for a repair job. He has presented several members of his family who have testified that they saw him pay you in cash when you finished the job. I must decide . . ."

"Your honor," the plaintiff interrupted, "I don't care if I lose. But to show you what liars the defendant and his family are, I never even finished the job."

WHAT DO YOU DO WHEN YOU AND THE CONTRACTOR can't see eye to eye? Basically, there are two time periods when you and the contractor can have disputes: while the job is being done or after it is finished. Let's take them in order.

Disputes During the Work

Okay, you've tried everything, and the work is not going the way you planned. The house is a mess at the end of the day. Your backyard looks like Baghdad after Operation Desert Storm. The work is running behind schedule. The wrong tiles are in place halfway around the bathroom. The skylights are installed all wrong. And you're unhappy with the lighting that the contractor designed. What do you do? You start by talking.

When I was unhappy with the sawdust that was all over the paved parking area in back of our home each day, I told the contractor that I expected it to be cleaned up, especially because the sawdust was blowing into my organic vegetable garden. I could tell that he wasn't thrilled with my request, but he complied. No problem.

I had recommended this same contractor to my friends, who had a large amount of renovation done to their townhouse condominium. My friends were thinking of having a lighting designer come in for the job. But the contractor assured them that he could take care of lighting design along with a designer who worked with his firm. As it turned out, my friends were not happy with part of his design, and the electrical subcontractor moved the offending locations. This turned out to be a disastrous move. None of the fixtures then correctly illuminated the areas they were supposed to. So my friends decided to call in a designer after all. By this time, some of the original cartons for the trim pieces had been thrown away, and the pieces were covered with dust. They could not be returned to the supplier. So costs went up. And my friends *think* they ended up paying the general contractor for his lighting design time.

Overall, they were very happy with the remodeler's performance. But my friends let him know that they felt that all the parties involved played a part in "blowing" the lighting phase of the project. The additional cost of the electrician was worked out between the remodeler and the electrician. My friends are not sure who paid for the unreturnable trim pieces because their costs went up anyway when they ultimately upgraded the fixtures.

For sure, the contractor did not charge for extra work by the electrical sub. And my friends feel that they did not pay substantially more for all the redesign and reinstallation than they would have paid had they hired a lighting consultant to begin with. What is the lesson here?

Things can, and will, go wrong. The key is to find a way to resolve such problems without too much conflict or grief. What my friends did was deal with the contractor in a direct but diplomatic way. He took responsibility for the problems caused by the electrical sub's initiative. He didn't attempt to add on costs for having to work with the lighting consultant's designs in the middle of the job. My friends are easygoing and didn't demand a cost analysis for all the fixtures and related parts and for the contractor's original lighting design. Had they made such a demand they might have fought for even more savings.

During this same renovation, a skylight was added to the stairwell. The city building inspector determined that the smoke detector in the hallway adjacent to the skylight was no longer adequate because the skylight created a higher point inside the hallway. A smoke detector at a higher location was called for. The remodeler had a new hardwire smoke detector—a smoke detector that is connected to the house electrical wiring by an electrician—installed just under the skylight and added $75 to my friends' bill. When my friend learned of this she told the contractor that she needed to vent her dissatisfaction about this arrangement and that once she got it off her chest she would feel better. She felt that the contractor should have known that raising the ceiling would necessitate relocating the detector and that the cost of doing so should, therefore, have been included in the original estimate and contract. The contractor, without hesitation, offered to deduct the price of the detector. My friend turned down the offer. She was satisfied with his having taken responsibility.

Was this an ideal situation, or what? It is what Herb Cohen refers to as a Win-Win negotiation in his book *You Can Negotiate Anything.* Both the homeowner and the contractor got what they wanted. But now we must deal with less-than-ideal conflict. What if the remodeler had told my friends to take the smoke detector and shove it up their skylight? And what if he'd insisted on being paid for the original lighting design *and* for the first batch of recessed lighting trim *and* for the culpable electrician's extra time *and* for having to adapt the work to the lighting designer's new specs?

The homeowners could refuse to make the next scheduled payment until the work was done to their satisfaction. In which case the contractor could refuse to continue with the work. Or he could file for a mechanic's lien. Or he could start screwing up on the job or abandon it outright.

We can speculate forever. So let's look at some examples of problems and how to approach solutions. Let's go back to the example I gave previously of a bathroom halfway tiled with the wrong tiles. Above all, you are entitled to satisfaction. That is the reason we make contracts—to assure that both sides will get what they agreed to. If Contractor Connie tries to make you feel that you are being petty, or if she tries to play on your emotions by saying that this is just a minor mistake and that pulling up all the tiles and purchasing the correct ones and having the tiler reinstall them will cost her a lot of money that she cannot afford right now because her daughter is about to enter an expensive college, just remember that it is not your responsibility to make up for her inadequacies.

You may decide that you are willing to work out a compromise. Perhaps the contractor will compensate for the wrong wall tiles by upgrading or redesigning the floor tiles. Maybe she will throw in a tub enclosure or give you fabulous above-the-tile wall covering or an extra built-in cabinet. If some such arrangement would please you, you and the contractor will avoid making each other miserable. But this does not mean you *should* make such an arrangement. If nothing but the original tile will put a smile on your puss, don't let the contractor's frustration dissuade you from having your dream come true. You probably work hard for your income (I'm assuming you're not Ed McMahon), and you deserve your money's worth.

But what do you do in a situation wherein the remodeler becomes Countess Dracula and starts sucking the life out of you? Do you bargain with, threaten, fire, or sue her? To a large degree this depends on how rigid she is and how able and willing your own personality allows you to be. Some people would rather be ripped off or intimidated than face the anxiety of conflict. If you are a person who is fearful of such situations, you must summon the courage to put your foot down and insist on getting what you are paying for and what you have a right to expect as a result of your contract negotiations. There are many cases, some of which will be described in Chapter 7, in which remodelers are called in to correct work that was started by an incompetent or dishonest fellow remodeler. You must decide when to cut your losses and move on—possibly seeking redress of damages through the legal system.

Let's take the case of a remodeling job wherein the carpenter installs cabinets in the kitchen. When that phase of the job is finished, the homeowner looks it over and discovers that instead of the cabinets being solid wood, only the doors are real wood. The rest of the "boxes" are composed of particle board with matching veneer on the outside, and the backs are simply a compositon material covered with a wood-grain print. The homeowners specified all-hardwood cabinets because they wanted quality. Particle board needs to be painted or it will swell when wet. Veneers can separate. The homeowner tells the contractor that the cabinets will have to go.

"Are you crazy?" responds the contractor. "If I rip out the cabinets, I'll have to patch and paint the walls. And I don't know if I can get a refund from the supply house. Then I'll have to order custom solid-wood cabinets. That'll take a few weeks. And it'll cost a lot more money. I won't be able to install the appliances until the new cabinets are in. And the whole job will be set back. No way. This is what you get."

Let's look at your options. You can let the remodeler know that you have a contract which includes all the details and that the cabinets are deficient. You will not make another payment until the contractor makes good. You can work out a compromise if that is a realistic option. You can demand arbitration or mediation (more on this coming up). You can call a lawyer for help. You can fire the contractor. Or you can just give in. That last one is no option at all. If you will not be happy with anything but the agreed-upon cabinets . . . get those cabinets!

It is up to you to decide how far you are willing to take the conflict. Think it over. Study the options. Talk to your family or friends. If you must have it your way, and the contractor is not willing to comply, resolve yourself to conflict and forge ahead. Having an attorney contact the contractor to represent you may move things closer to being worked out. It's worth a try.

If the work is partially completed, you must decide whether or not to let the work continue while the dispute is ongoing. Before you make this decision, consider how much of a negative impact it could have on your life. If there is a wall missing and winter is just around the corner, you may not want to stop work while you try to resolve the problem. On the other hand, you don't want to give contractors the impression that although you are miffed you are going to allow work to continue normally. If they have you over a barrel, I suggest you take this approach: While you are pursuing solutions to the dispute, write a letter and tell the remodeler that you expect work to go ahead but that you are seeking a resolution to the dispute and that you will make payments but that final payment will be withheld until the dispute is ultimately resolved by whatever means are provided for in the contract. Make sure that you send the letter by either registered or certified mail. Be sure that it is sent "return receipt requested." (This requires the recipient to sign for the mail upon delivery, and the signature is your proof that the letter was received.)

If the contractor refuses to sign for the letter, here is a little trick: Use the return address of a friend or relative. This way the remodeler does not know that the letter is coming from you and is much more likely to sign for it. When your friend receives the signed return receipt have that person turn it over to you with an affidavit stating that the receipt was for *your* letter and that he or she read its contents before mailing it. This could be valuable evidence for a future lawsuit or arbitration proceeding. It establishes that you did not stand in the way of continuing progress on the job.

But let's suppose that going ahead with the work would require a decision. If the plumbing is all messed up, you can't go ahead and finish the wall and tile it. You can't attach the bathroom fixtures. If you stop work, you may lose the contractor altogether (which could be a blessing). Then the two of you would have to work out a settlement for work completed or go to arbitration.

And then, once again, you would have to go through the process of selecting a new remodeler to finish the job. This could entail the expense of redoing the first contractor's work. I cannot fully explain when and how to make the appropriate decision. The variables are infinite. But I will reiterate this tip: Let your guts be your guide. If you are getting the feeling that you should stop work—stop it. Regroup your thoughts and then decide what to do. Don't build your dream house on a foundation of quicksand.

You might even be threatened by a lawsuit from the contractor. Don't let such a situation scare you. If you've negotiated your contract as described in Chapter 3, you are entitled by the terms you drew up to have your case decided by arbitration.

If you do decide to stop work and you then incur additional expenses in order to correct the work done by the first contractor, you may have redress in law. If the first contractor's work was obviously below industry standards, that person may be obligated to pay for the corrective work done by the follow-up contractor. The problem may arise when you try to collect.

Another point over which disputes commonly arise is after "substantial performance." At this point, the contractor will expect her next-to-last payment. But what if you feel that the work is *not* substantially completed? *Black's Law Dictionary* defines "substantial performance" as existing "where there has been no willful departure from the terms of the contract, and no omission in essential points, and the contract has been honestly and faithfully performed in its materials and substantial particulars, and the only variance from the strict and literal performance consists of technical or unimportant omissions or defects." In other words, if the job is completed, except that the electrical outlet cover plates haven't been installed because they're on back order, you must make the appropriate payment, minus the cost of the deficient materials and labor. Don't forget, however, that you provided in your contract for *final* payment to be due only after the time limit for mechanics' lien notices expires.

Easier said than done. Is it substantial performance if you've had a pool installed in your backyard but the pump and filter have not been installed because the supplier is out of stock? What about a situation in which an attic has been upgraded but the whole-house fan hasn't been installed because of a defective part? These situations require either a willingness to compromise on the parts of the homeowners and contractor or the aid of a mediator, arbitrator, or judge. I will discuss the use of these dispute-resolution services later in this chapter.

Disputes After Completion

It is my sincere hope—and belief—that you will never have to use this section of the book. If you have followed my advice up until this point, you will be dealing with reliable professionals who take pride in their professionalism and who stand behind their work. They aim to please their customers.

However, sometimes disputes arise after contractors and their workers are gone. Mechanical parts fail, Formica peels, walls crack, security alarms go off when they're not supposed to. And sometimes it gets a lot worse. A pipe seam cracks and the water destroys a new hardwood floor. A swimming pool cracks, and the water leaks out and causes a mudslide on a downhill neighbor's property. A new step cracks, causing a visitor to fall and crack her head. And she sues. A summer and winter go by and all of a sudden the new windows can't be opened—not even a crack.

In each case, the homeowner approaches the remodeler and seeks correction of the problem. Or, in the case of the broken step, the homeowner seeks redress of the problem caused by the visitor's lawsuit. If the remodeler denies responsibility to make good, the homeowners are left holding the bag. But keep in mind that:

- You are dealing with a licensed contractor (in those states that adequately regulate).
- Your contract provides for a thorough warranty of the contractor's work and materials.
- Your contract provides for arbitration.
- If your contract doesn't provide for arbitration, there are mediation services available to you, as well as civil court. For small claims there is—guess what—small claims court.

The first step to take is to approach the remodeler with a reminder that the reason there is a warranty in the contract is precisely to relieve the homeowner of the trouble and expense of faulty work and/or materials. You would never have hired the remodeler had it not been for the fact that the contract provides for a very specific warranty. And since part of the work failed, it is up to the contractor to make good on it. Considering that the contractor you have chosen had to meet a series of criteria and "tests" before being selected for the job, it is likely that he or she would be a reasonable person about meeting his or her obligations.

But it is my objective to help you deal with the exceptional catastrophe, the one in which you are having difficulty in finding a resolution of your grievance. All people are defensive to *some* degree. And even the best of contractors can feel that any complaint about their work is a personal affront to their competence. Work around it. Attach no blame to the failure of the contractor. A spoonful of sugar makes the medicine go down. Allow the remodeler to make all the excuses in the world to defend herself. As long as she feels that you are not trying to milk an expression of guilt out of her, she is less likely to feel defensive and more likely to be willing to right the wrong.

But the possibility still exists that the contractor will not own up to her responsibility, especially in cases that would require substantial financial outlay, such as the one in which the pipe crack led to damaged wood flooring. When thousands of dollars are involved, it is human nature to find the hidden "truth" that exonerates us from responsibility. So despite your best diplomatic efforts, you may still be stuck with a stubborn contractor.

Mediation

Before you go to the mat with a contractor, suggest a way out of your conflict. Almost every community has a little secret available to its residents. That secret is mediation services, which are usually available for little or no cost. Some communities have separate volunteer programs. The rest provide mediation services through local bar associations. San Francisco is one of the pioneer cities in the area of community mediation. Its Community Board Program trains ordinary community volunteers in mediation techniques. It offers nonbinding mediation that helps the parties reach agreement in a peaceful atmosphere.

Local bar associations often offer mediation services as well. They provide the conflicting parties with the opportunity to air their grievances in a controlled atmosphere. The mediators do not take sides. As with the community programs, they seek a common ground upon which reconciliation can be built (it sounds like marriage counseling). The Better Business Bureaus, too, offer mediation programs that are conducted by ordinary folks who volunteer and are trained by BBB staffers.

The difficult part of this type of mediation is that both of the opposing parties must volunteer to participate. Once you've reached that point, the good part is that because you are both volunteering, the atmosphere is set for a conciliatory proceeding—unlike situations in which one party drags another into a legal confrontation.

In these mediation situations, the programs will get in touch with the contractor for you and try to convince him or her to participate. Such service helps you avoid the uncomfortable effort of trying to convince the contractor to submit him- or herself to such an effort. It's worth a try. You can always move on to more-binding proceedings if mediation fails.

You can find mediation services listed in your yellow pages under "Mediation Services," or you can call the local bar association. In addition, many small claims court jurisdictions offer mediation or arbitration services that can help the contending parties avoid an ugly court battle.

Warranty Programs

If you contracted with the remodeler to have her provide an independent warranty program, such as Home Owners Warranty (HOW), your problems may be answered. (I am not, however, endorsing Home Owners Warranty over any other provider.) If the source of your dispute is that the work or materials provided by the remodeler failed, you can take your gripe directly to the warranty provider.

You will have to check whether your particular warranty agency provides dispute-resolution services. HOW provides an informal dispute-settlement system that has leverage with its subscriber contractors. Contractors who are not being reasonable can be dropped by HOW. It does, in theory, carefully screen its contractor members. HOW deals strictly with builders and remodelers, not with specialty contractors. You will find that true of any warranty service. Plumbers and carpenters on their own would not normally subscribe to such programs.

But what if such dispute-settlement efforts do not work? Seek payment from the insurance program. Did I say "insurance"? That's exactly what warranty programs are. They insure the work done by subscriber contractors. You might want to review the discussion of HOW's warranty program on pages 44–45.

Other outfits also insure remodelers' work. Some are regional. If during the negotiating stage your contractor offers you *any* insurance program, check out its credentials with your local contractors' trade organizations, Better Business Bureau, department of consumer affairs, or attorney general's or city attorney's office. With adequate coverage, you don't have to worry about even confronting a recalcitrant contractor.

Here's how HOW arranges the settlement. Its insurance division sends an adjuster to the site. The adjuster will make a determination of the damage. If the problem arose during the first two years of the warranty, the adjuster will make a determination of what the remodeler needs to do to correct the work. Beyond two years, the adjuster will determine what the fair market cost of rectifying the problem should be. For more complex situations, the adjuster may call in an engineer to determine what remedies are called for. Then, depending on a series of variables, HOW will either assign another contractor to do the corrective work or it will pay the homeowner, who may then seek a suitable contractor.

Arbitration

Okay, so you don't have a warranty policy to fall back on. And even though your contractor was great all the way through the project, after the job she has turned out to be a defensive creep. So now what do you do? Yep . . . arbitration! You have to call in your marker and play your hand. But that's why you insisted on having a provision for this type of dispute settlement in your contract.

Bear in mind that this can be a two-way street. It is possible that the contractor will have a claim against you because you withheld payment based upon your dissatisfaction with work for which he or she was responsible.

Some of the warranty insurance providers also furnish arbitration services. HOW provides arbitration for claims during the first two years of the warranty. Its participating remodelers are responsible for correcting problems during that period. If they fail to perform, the homeowner may make a request to HOW for dispute settlement. The warranty company then contacts the National Academy of Conciliators, which hears the case and then makes a decision that is binding on the remodeler *but not on the homeowner*. A homeowner who isn't happy with the arbitration ruling is free to seek the next means of dispute settlement, including a separate arbitration agency as provided for in the contract.

In 1988 the American Arbitration Association heard nearly 5,000 construction cases that involved contracts totaling $786 million.

You will have to get in touch with the arbitration service designated in the contract. It will set up a hearing date for you and the contractor that is convenient for you both. During that time you must prepare. Remember, you have agreed in advance to be bound by arbitration. If you go into the proceeding unprepared and with a casual attitude, you will stand a poor chance of establishing your argument and winning your case. A contractor can show up with witnesses you never heard of to say that they saw you interfere or that you said something that you never even dreamed of.

The preparations and precautions I will list apply to any binding dispute-settlement proceeding, whether it be arbitration, small claims court, or regular civil court (however, in regular civil court you will usually be represented by an attorney). Accumulate all of the material evidence possible. Remember that accordion file I told you to keep all of the records of the project in? It's your first resource. It is where you have kept the signed agreements, the records of phone conversations, the lien releases, and the proofs of payments.

But is it enough? Probably not. How can you prove assertions about the quality of the work, the mistakes that were made, the craftsmanship that failed? With witnesses, photographs, and repairpersons—particularly those who had to go in and fix what the contractor's people screwed up. When the job is finished and the work fails after a period of time, there are usually witnesses. If you have no family, call up friends and neighbors. Show them the damage. Make sure that they remember the problems for such time as they might be witnesses. And take lots of pictures. Make sure that they're clear. Put a ruler next to the problem area in the photo if dimensions are important to your case.

And rehearse your argument. Know what you want to say. Study the facts. Remember the sequence of events that led to the conflict. Then organize the evidence. You don't want to have to go fishing around when you're trying to present your argument to the arbitrator. Try not to be nervous when you go into the hearing. Follow the procedures as laid down by the arbitrator. Try not to be argumentative or contentious. Don't interrupt, yell, or lose your cool.

Regulatory Agencies

In addition to the dispute-resolution resources that I've just delineated, there are several possible ways to seek resolution of your grievance through the use of governmental and private agencies.

The Better Business Bureau in your area will handle your complaint. Call or write for a complaint form. File your complaint by mail and keep your fingers crossed. If the BBB cannot resolve your complaint directly with the contractor, it will at least keep a record of it on file so that the next time someone calls with an inquiry about that contractor, the BBB can inform that person that there is an unresolved complaint outstanding. That potential customer, if as sharp as you were, will avoid hiring that contractor. Revenge is better than nothing. And remember, the BBB also offers arbitration in disputes that involve its members. The decision is binding only on the member business—not on the consumer. And it offers nonbinding mediation for any parties that request it.

Each state that regulates contractors (see Appendix A) has an agency that deals with the contractor. You must file a complaint and ask that the regulatory agency investigate the complaint. By using the threat of pulling the contractor's license, the agency may be able to get you satisfaction. The effectiveness of such regulatory agencies varies widely. In California, the Contractors' State License Board has a spotty record. Its reputation is for dragging its feet and not being hard enough on wayward contractors. My own experience bears this out. If you feel that your complaint is not receiving the attention and advocacy it deserves, make noise! Remember The Rule of the Psychological Hump. Dog the bureaucrats until they take action. And make sure that the complaint is kept on record for future inquiries.

If you hired a contractor who belongs to a professional trade association, you should file for dispute resolution with that association first, providing that it will not delay having your case heard in court to a time past the expiration of the statute of limitations. This is a "friendly" recourse that contractors have allowed for by letting their customers know that they belong to an organization that provides such a service. It's one of their selling points. The attempt at conflict resolution is administered by *the contractor's* organization. It could be difficult for contractors to resist arbitration or mediation with their own trade association and still remain members in good standing.

Virtually every city, country, and state has at least one regulatory agency that deals with consumer affairs. Los Angeles County, for example, has a department of consumer affairs. So does the state of California. Both are found in the separate governmental listings in the front section of the white pages telephone directory. The Contractors' State License Board is listed there as well. In addition, the regular alphabetical listings contain the heading "Consumer Complaints and Information." That listing contains dozens of state regulatory agencies for various occupations and professions—each with its own phone number.

In California, a homeowner who has a complaint will be referred by the department of consumer affairs to the Contractors' State License Board. This is unfortunate because of its less-than-stellar reputation.

In fact, California has a highly evolved consumer protection framework that works well at least part of the time. Your own state may do as well or better. If it doesn't, there are other governmental resources you can try.

Each state has an attorney general's office. Attorneys general (yup, that is the correct plural) are given the responsibility for enforcing their states' criminal laws. If you feel that you have been victimized by a contractor who has committed fraud or who has run a scam on you, call the attorney general's office. The "scam" falls under the heading of a crime, but not every dispute involves a scam.

Your city attorney's office or district attorney may be able to help as well.

Small Claims Court

Going to small claims court can actually be a fun adventure. It's exciting, but low-key. It's quick. It's informal. But it's the real thing. If you've never litigated in small claims court, you might want to spend a morning, afternoon, or evening there, observing the goings-on. It's free, it's fun, and you'll learn the ropes for possible future use. I have been a plaintiff there many times myself. One time I was even a defendant. I lost three times. On two of the three occasions I lost—it is my true belief—because the "judge" did not adjudicate in a proper manner. In short, if the hearing officer (I'll explain later why I do not necessarily use the term "judge") performs according to the rules of law, you stand an excellent chance of prevailing.

Each state has its own procedures, financial limits, and regulations. Contact the small claims adviser or court clerk for a synopsis of state small claims regulations. Remember that small claims court is limited to *small claims*. That means if you are making a claim for $25,000, you're in the wrong place. And if your contract calls for arbitration in case of any controversies, you have no right to go to court. Some contract arbitration provisions, however, allow for small claims court litigation for those amounts that do not exceed local limitations. That limitation may vary from as little as $1,000 to as much as $7,000, depending on the state you live in. You can look up your local court in the government listings of your telephone directory.

I advise that before you embark on a small claims procedure you write a formal, polite, counciliatory letter to the contractor. Explain in detail why you feel you have something coming and what that something is. Do not address the letter, "Dear Moldy-Oatmeal-for-Brains: I hope that your business fails and that the grief gives you a heart attack. . . ." Send the letter by certified mail with a return receipt requested. When you get the signed receipt, you will be able to show in court that you tried to be decent about seeking a solution on the outside. (Save a copy of the letter as well.) It may or may not have some influence with the judge.

Here's how small claims court works. You go to the court clerk's office and fill out a form (make sure that you bring the contractor's business name, the owner's actual name, the business address, and the phone number). You then select a trial—or hearing—date and arrange for the summons to be served upon the defendant (that's the contractor). If this sounds like a lot of work to you—surprise! It isn't. The process is usually simple, straightforward, and not very time-consuming. So don't be intimidated.

And if you have never been party to a trial, I assure you that usually the small claims trial process is relatively painless. The informal nature of the proceeding and its brevity make for a relatively rapid and uncomplicated court confrontation. If you have ever watched "The People's Court," you have a rough idea of the style of the hearing. Some judges are more stern than Judge Wapner. Most are softer and less intimidating. So unless you are having major self-esteem problems, I advise you to set your anxieties aside and just go in armed with the truth and a positive attitude.

Many courts even offer arbitration or mediation services. You might want to inquire and see if your small claims court does. In addition, many courts, particularly those in larger cities, offer a small claims adviser service that helps potential litigants through the process by explaining the rules and regulations. If not, the court clerk's office usually bears that responsibility.

Remember that you are limited in the amount of your claim. In California, the claim limit is $5,000. But if you feel that the contractor screwed up two or more unconnected parts of the job, you may sue for each offense separately on the same court date. You will have to pay a separate fee—usually under $15—for each suit. This fee is normally refundable to you by the defendant if you win the trial. You can sue once, let's say, for a defective bay window installation, and once more for improperly installing a wall oven.

When you file with the court clerk, you will receive several copies of the court papers. You can either have them served upon the defendant by someone you know, by a process server, by registered mail, or by a marshall or sheriff (depending upon which agency handles it in your area). I strongly recommend that you use such a law-enforcement agency for serving the court papers. The defendant is very unlikely to try to resist service from a uniformed official. The deputy is experienced at this type of work and will usually make several attempts to deliver, even if it means attempting service before the sun comes up (which, of course, means nothing to folks in Alaska). Again, you pay a fee for this service. But it too is reimbursable if you win in court. And it costs the offending s.o.b. even more than just the damages! Incidentally, contractors are often not in their offices because they are out working. So if you have their home addresses, the service of the court papers can be made at home.

Because you signed the contract at your home (you did, didn't you?) the court that serves your home area is the place to file. Contractors have to come to your neighborhood. Serves them right.

Don't wait too long to file. Statutes of limitations limit the amount of time you have to file your suit. Such statutes vary from state to state and by category of lawsuit. If the incident in question occurred more than a year earlier, call your local court clerk or small claims adviser to find out which statute applies to your case. If you are still not sure, file the suit and let the judge make the determination. Another reason you should file promptly is that defendants could move away or go out of business before you get to them. Note also that if the contractor's business is incorporated, you have to sue the corporation. The contractor's liability is limited to the business itself, and it is difficult, though not impossible, to sue the individual who ran the corporation.

When we purchased our home, it was understood—and the law required—that hardwire smoke detectors would be installed by the seller in each bedroom and in the hallway. More than four years later we discovered that two of the detectors were battery operated and that they would probably have failed in a fire because the batteries were old. The seller refused to pay to have the proper detectors installed. As a matter of fact, he told me exactly what type of sexual encounter to have with myself. And then he said the wrong words: "Sue me!" So I did. Although the suit was filed beyond the period normally allowed by the statute of limitations, the judge allowed the suit because the fraud was not discovered until years after it took place. The battery-operated detectors constituted a "latent defect," that is, a defect that was hidden. The statute of limitations was thereby extended. I won. The seller paid.

How large a judgment should you seek? There are two ways to determine this amount. You can sue for the amount you paid the contractor for the phase or phases of the job that was screwed up. Or you can sue to have the work redone. Sometimes a botched job can cost more to remove and replace than the cost of starting a job from scratch. To prove to the court that you will be incurring this extra cost, you may have to ask for written estimates from other contractors and then bring these estimates to court as evidence. In some cases, the damage is so serious that it must be corrected almost immediately. A chimney that is on the verge of collapse, a foundation that is sinking, or an unfinished outer wall when Thanksgiving has just passed and you live in Vermont could mean that the job has to be finished by replacement contractors regardless of how litigation may turn out. The cost of such corrective work is easy to prove in court and will go far toward making your case.

In small claims court it is almost always futile to seek compensation for pain and suffering you may have suffered as a result of the culpability or stupidity of the contractor. Such claims usually go further in civil court than they do in the small claims division. Unless you can prove that consequential damages were an inevitable result of the contractor's negligence or incompetence, you will have trouble collecting for such consequential losses. The example I gave earlier of a broken pipe destroying hardwood floors would most likely be the responsibility of the contractor in any court—providing that the pipe's breaking was due to poor work on the part of the contractor's employees. It might even be covered by the contractor's liability insurance.

A word about default judgments: whew! There is a good chance that the defendant will fail to show up in court. It is estimated that a third of all defendants are no-shows. If that happens in your case, consider yourself on your opponent's one-yard line, first down, and you need only one point to win the game. So don't fumble! The judge is likely to ask you to state your case. And unless your argument is without merit, he or she will decide in your favor—a *default judgment*. I did once witness a person talk himself right out of a default judgment because he talked too much and started to give the other guy's side of the story.

A word about lawyers: Most states do not allow plaintiffs to be represented by attorneys in small claims court. Those that do are probably not doing you any favors. If you are capable of following the principles in this book, you can do just as well representing yourself unless you have severe insecurity problems, fear of speaking to authority figures, or agoraphobia. In such cases, the judge will allow you to have a friend or relative there with you to do the talking as a sort of interpreter.

If you live in a state in which the defendant is allowed to have an attorney, don't be intimidated if one is present. If you are well prepared and present your case in a clear, forthright manner, the judge is likely not to be swayed by the presence of an attorney.

Bear in mind that a judge does not want to hear every minute detail of every conversation that ever took place between you and the contractor. Limit your argument to the salient points. Present your evidence as you go through your argument, making sure to present the photographs at the right moment. Be sure that they are clearly labeled on the back. The judge will guide you through the arguments. Address him and don't get involved in arguments with your opponent.

Evidence of loss could include repair bills, signed repair estimates, canceled checks, and even medical bills. If the inadequate work has already been repaired, be sure that you have before-and-after photos. And bring the contract and any relevant change orders and lien releases.

Witnesses are a definite plus—eyewitnesses to the work or damage, witnesses to conversations between you and the contractor, or expert witnesses who are professionals and who have expertise in the area of contention. It is often difficult, however, to get witnesses to come to court, especially during working hours. For that reason you might want to get an evening court date. Written witness testimony will often be considered if the affidavit is signed, dated, and clearly written.

I strongly recommend that you practice your presentation at home. And keep it short. On "The People's Court" Judge Wapner is often seen telling the litigants to get to the point or cutting them off so that he can ask essential questions. At my job as the "Consumer Watch" reporter at KFSN-TV in Fresno, I often receive calls from people who need help but who cannot stick to the point and present their situation in a clear and concise way. They bring up all kinds of irrelevant problems. What they need for those issues is a counselor. They have trouble sticking to answering my questions. I have neither the time nor the patience for such meanderings. Imagine what it's like being a judge who hears twenty or more cases a day. They don't have time for extraneous yammering.

But don't be intimidated by court officials. Some are warm and helpful. Others are incompetent jerks. Assume an air of confidence and be very polite.

The ins and outs of small claims court are too involved to get into here. Ask your local court clerk's office or small claims adviser to provide you with a pamphlet about small claims procedures. A point that should be covered in the pamphlet is what to do in case the defendant counter-claims. In contracting disputes, this would most likely be in the form of claims for unpaid bills.

Settlements often are reached outside the courtroom just before the trial is about to commence. In such a case, I recommend that you get paid and that you have a written, signed settlement agreement that covers all the loopholes. The settlement should include the case number, the date, and the amount of the settlement. And don't trust the other party. Ask the clerk to move your case to the end of the calendar while you work out the details. If you have the case dismissed in exchange for the settlement and then you are not paid or the check bounces, you will have to go through the process all over again. If you have been paid by check, call the defendant's bank to see that there are sufficient funds to cover it. After you have recorded the settlement with the clerk, go immediately to the defendant's bank and cash the check.

If the defendant asks for a continuance—a delay of trial—it is usually a harassment tactic. Oppose it. Politely tell the judge that the defendant had plenty of time to ask for a delay before the trial date; that you had already requested mediation and that you cannot afford to keep rearranging your schedule; and that the same applies to your witnesses. The rest is up to the judge.

If a court officer announces that your case will be heard by a judge pro tem (temporary judge) or a referee, I advise you to request that your case be heard by the sitting judge. Judges pro tem are usually neophyte judges-in-training who often don't know what they're doing in spite of what you are told about their qualifications by court officers. However, I will say that the last case I was involved in was heard by a commissioner who was so nasty and incompetent that I regretted not going with the pro tem I had just avoided. The commissioner was so incompetent, in fact, that I filed a formal complaint against him with the presiding judge of the municipal court.

The verdict may be appealed if the defendant loses. Many jurisdictions do not allow appeals on the part of plaintiffs. They don't occur very often because they are usually not worth the trouble. However, if you lose and you feel that the verdict was ridiculous, consider an appeal if one is allowed. The clerk of the court can provide you with more information.

Collecting the judgment is the tough part. If the defendant fails to pay within the allotted time, it will be up to you to pursue the matter. It is an unfortunate condition of small claims court that you have to go through hell and high water (which is just a little worse than going through Reno) in order to get the court to help you enforce the judgment against the defendant. It will be up to you to locate the contractor's property, vehicles, bank accounts, office funishings, and the like. If you are unable to do that, you will have to get the court to subpoena the contractor to court in order to have him or her disclose the whereabouts of resources. Once these facts are known, you can sic the marshals on the contractor, whose property they can confiscate.

If the contractor is not incorporated, you can go after her personal property, home, and bank accounts. *You* may even place a lien on the *contractor's* property. If you want to stop the defendant from unloading resources before you can get to her, you can get an "abstract of judgment" from the court and take it to the appropriate county records office in order to put a lien on the property. This precludes the property from being sold in much the same way that a mechanic's lien prevents the transfer of your property until the debt is paid.

If the defendant fails to show up to divulge resources, you are finally in a position to have the court issue a contempt citation and then issue a bench warrant for her arrest.

I want to remind you that this chapter is relevant to you only in the rare case wherein you have come to the gates of contractor "hell." If you have followed the advice of the previous chapters, you should not run into such difficulties, because you have chosen a reliable professional and you have protected yourself from most of the unfortunate contingencies that might occur.

Lawyers

If *all* else fails, it's time for you to consult a lawyer. If the contractor has gotten away with violating your contractual agreement, you may want to take him or her to civil court. Find a lawyer by first seeking the recommendations of acquaintances (sound familiar?) who have had successful experiences with civil attorneys whom they trust.

Things to Remember

1. If you feel that the work is not going satisfactorily, express yourself clearly to the contractor, who may be willing to offer restitution.

2. If the contractor doesn't offer to right the wrong, ask for corrective action. Be polite but firm.

3. If a solution is not forthcoming, consider withholding payment until contract requirements are met.

4. If the work in question is important to the outcome of other work yet to be done, stop all work, if possible, until the conflict is resolved.

5. Seek mediation through your community conflict-resolution service, bar association, or department of consumer affairs.

6. If the contractor is unwilling to participate in mediation, try the professional trade association to which she belongs. It should offer mediation or arbitration. If the contractor doesn't have such membership but does carry a warranty program, see if the warranty company offers arbitration.

7. If none of the above works out, seek binding arbitration under the terms of the contract.

8. If the work's expeditious completion is an urgent need, you may have to consider firing the contractor and seeking an outside contractor to finish the job A.S.A.P.

9. Don't make the next-to-last payment until you are sure that you have received "substantial performance."

10. If, after the job has been completed and you have made final payment, something goes wrong, politely but firmly ask the contractor to correct the problem.

11. If your contractor provided an independent warranty program, it's time to cash in your chips and enforce the warranty.

12. If the contractor is not willing to honor his or her obligations, seek mediation through one of the services outlined above.

13. If neither of these approaches works, enforce the arbitration provision of your contract.

14. If your contractor acted in an unethical or illegal way, seek help from private or governmental agencies. The Better Business Bureau, state licensing agency, department of consumer affairs, attorney general's office, and city attorney's office are places to start.

15. If you left an arbitration clause out of the contract (shame on you!) and the loss is relatively small, consider taking your case to small claims court. Your arbitration clause may allow for small claims court anyway.

16. Regardless of which dispute-settlement course you take, prepare carefully for your hearing. Gather paper evidence, photographs, and expert and eyewitnesses. Rehearse your argument. Be familiar with the proceedings in which you will be taking part.

17. Don't wait too long to file your claim. A statute of limitations could shut you out.

18. If a settlement is offered before the trial or arbitration proceeding, consider it. But protect yourself before you allow your case to be dismissed.

19. If the defendant fails to honor the judgment, you will have to follow certain procedures in order to collect. The court clerk or small claims adviser service can help you with information on how to enforce the judgment.

7

Scams and Nightmares

The door-to-door salesman was speaking to the homeowner. "If you give me a deposit right now, I can secure ownership of the Eiffel Tower for you for $10,000."

"Listen, you crook, I'm not a fool," responded the homeowner. "I already bought it last week . . . and I paid only five grand for it."

THE PURPOSE OF THIS CHAPTER IS TO HELP YOU STEER clear of the traps and pitfalls that are being set up by the outlaws and unethical practitioners who want your money . . . no matter what. The chapter is divided into two sections: the scams that crooks use to get between you and your money, and a few true nightmares that have been inflicted on naive or unsuspecting homeowners because they didn't carefully go about protecting themselves or because they didn't listen to their guts.

Scams

The purpose of this section is to drive home the point that professionals who come to your home uninvited and who then try to convince you to have work done that you did not request are, at best, big risks. At worst, they're ruthless crooks. Following are some examples.

Driveway Sleight of Hand

A gentleman rings your doorbell and says that he noticed that there are cracks in your driveway. He says that he and his crew have just finished a job in the neighborhood and since they have some driveway sealer left over and they just happened to be driving by, they will be willing to redo your driveway at a very low cost—say $50. You agree to the deal, and he goes to get his men. They show up and start unloading the cans of driveway sealer. The "contractor" then says, "Okay, that's gonna be ten cans. So the whole job comes to $500." You thought it was $50 for the job. "Oh, you misunderstood," says the scammer. "I'll tell you what. As long as we're here already and the guys have started, I'll do the job for $400. But it'll have to be cash."

Most people won't have that kind of cash on hand, so the man volunteers to drive you to the bank. While you're away, the men do a slipshod job using cheap sealer . . . if you're lucky. If not, they will rob your home while you're busy with the con (and I don't mean *con*tractor) and take off before you know what hit you.

The lesson: Never have unsolicited work done. Never have work done without a contract. Don't pay until after you inspect the job. Know how to reach the contractor tomorrow. Check references.

The Paint Shell Game

You get bids from several painters and choose the one who offers the lowest price. The contract specifies a particular color and brand of paint. When the painter shows up he has one-gallon or five-gallon cans with the brand name on them. What you don't know is that instead of the brand you wanted, he has filled the cans with an inferior brand of paint and resealed the cans. Perhaps you think you are getting a durable, washable, fade-resistant paint. Instead, your house is being painted with a product that will not hold up well.

Although it is harder for the painter to fool you with an unusual color, it is easy to do with common colors like Navajo white. Make sure any novel colors match the paint chip you originally used to help you pick out the color.

Lesson: Look at all the paint cans and make sure that—except for one or two cans that may be left over from another job—they are clean and new-looking. The painter could start off with a couple of cans of the brand-name paint and then refill them from another can of the cheap stuff. Make sure you see enough empty brand-name cans to account for the whole job.

(And don't forget that paint and used cans are hazardous waste and should be disposed of properly.)

Big Job; Small Payments; Goodbye House

A scam that has recently been run in Los Angeles is one of the most heartless and insidious I have ever heard of. It is most commonly attempted in somewhat run-down areas populated by minorities. The scam artists, representing themselves as contractors, find homes that are in obvious need of repair. They then look up the county records on the properties to see which ones are owned outright by the owners, free and clear of bank loans. This information tells them that the occupants of the home have probably lived in it for decades and have paid off the mortgage. There will, therefore, be no interference from a bank.

The scamsters then attempt to find out if the property is occupied by a single elderly person—most likely a widow or widower. If so, they then attempt to convince the prospective victim that they could do necessary repairs for a very low price. The repairs might include siding, roofing, toilet-fixture replacement, paving, and the like. The more the victim allows the perpetrators to see of the home, the more things they could find wrong. They then offer the widow or widower a low monthly price to pay for the repair. They say something like, "The whole job will cost you only $150 per month for two years. Then there would be no more monthly payments." The unsuspecting victim gives an okay for the job. The scamsters draw up the papers and have the victim sign them.

The victim, of course, doesn't realize that buried in the endless paragraphs of small print is a requirement for a balloon payment of $30,000 due at the end of the two years. The debt would be secured by the property. The senior citizen has no way to pay off the exorbitant balance, and the crooks then attempt to foreclose on the debt. With a successful foreclosure, the property could be sold at market value and the "contractors" would attempt to pocket the excess proceeds above the $30,000 instead of forwarding all of the excess proceeds to the home-owner.

Lesson: Never trust a door-to-door contractor. If you are tempted to hire one, check references and check out the address of the business. Never sign a contract that you do not understand 100 percent. And if you are not good at fully comprehending such things, enlist the services of someone who does.

Termite Terrorists

A guy comes to your door and says that he is offering a free termite inspection—no obligation. He will check out your house, and if he finds nothing—fine. If he finds termites he will make a competitive bid. What the heck, you think, I've got nothing to lose. So the guy checks out your attic or under your house and . . . *voilà!* He comes up with a piece of two-by-four that's got enough holes in it to make Bonnie and Clyde look like they were killed by smothering. Wanna bet he took that board in with him?

He then offers an incredibly cheap price to rid your home of the pestilence. You ask him how he will treat it. He says that he will spray all exposed lumber within the structure. Baloney. Your home must either be treated with fumigation after it has been sealed or, if you are using a special alternative treatment, it must be thorough, licensed, and verifiable through references.

Lesson: Don't let solicitors into your home. If the offer sounds too good to be true after a suspicious inspection, call in a well-known outfit that offers free inspections to verify the solicitor's allegations. If they do hold up, check out the proposed method of treatment. Then go through the other procedures for verifying the reliability of the contractor, as described earlier.

Siding Loopholes

You respond to a mail promotion or door-to-door salesman and get an estimate to have the siding on your house replaced. Once the siding is installed, the salesman asks you whether you want the trim, eaves, and gutters done as well. To your surprise, there was nothing in the contract to cover them. You can say no and leave things as is, you can pay the cheat to do them, or you can call another contractor to finish the job. If you hesitate about saying yes to the salesman, he can say to you, "I can give you this price only if I put my men to work on it while they're still at your home. If they have to make another trip in a few days it'll cost ya."

Lesson: You know it already: Get *everything* in writing in advance. And check those references.

Skinny Drywall

No, the name of this section is not that of an obscure 1940s band leader. Drywall—also known as plasterboard and Sheetrock—is what interior house walls are most commonly made of today. It replaced the old plaster walls of years ago. It generally comes in three thicknesses: ⅜″, ½″, or ⅝″. The thicker the sheets of drywall, the better the temperature and sound insulation and the more resistance to an errant hammer. When I was the consumer reporter for the "Home" TV show, on ABC, we set up a contraption that simultaneously swung hammers with equal velocity into three pieces of drywall of the respective thicknesses. The hammer went right through the ⅜″ piece. It severely damaged the ½″ piece. The ⅝″ piece suffered only a small dent that was easily patched.

Contractors who replace ⅝″ drywall with ⅜″ sheets can pocket the money saved.

Bathrooms require a special type of drywall known as greenboard. The covering on greenboard is green (clever, eh?), and it's water-resistant in order to protect the enclosed plaster from absorbing hot-water vapors. If the contractor uses regular drywall in the bathroom, the material could swell in a few years.

Lesson: Specify ⅝″ drywall in your contract unless your contractor can give you a good reason not to. Specify greenboard for your bathroom. Check the material for compliance before it is installed. The actual specs of the drywall sheet are printed on the four-foot edges. (Each sheet is 4 feet wide.)

Useless Roof? Gimme Proof!

Water is leaking from your roof into your bedroom. You call a roofer, who tells you that your entire roof needs to be replaced. "Can't it just be patched?" you ask. The roofer smiles as if to say, "How cute and naive."

"No, no," is what the roofer actually says. "The decking under the roofing material is rotted out. If you patch one place you'll be patching another place in a few weeks. In the long run it will do more damage and cost you more money. You'll need to replace the decking. The job will cost about $10,000." When you regain consciousness, you decide not to be cheap about your own home. You go for it. The roofer was right. You are naive.

The solution would have been to get two or three other well-qualified roofers to give you estimates. They might have told you that an inexpensive patch job would be just what the doctor ordered.

Lesson: Get competitive bids from professionals who come highly recommended. If you know someone who had roofing work done *several years* ago and was happy with the job, you're off to a good start. A recent roofing job won't tell you how well the work stood up. It hasn't withstood the test of time.

The Furnace "Inspector"—He'll Make You Hot Under the Collar

A man comes to your door and says that he's doing free furnace safety inspections in your area. He may identify himself as a salesman, fire inspector, building inspector, gas-company official, or the like. He looks at your furnace and finds that it's in immediate need of repair. It could explode! Your family could be destroyed! Your neighborhood could disappear from the face of the Earth! He then tells you that he has to shut it off until it is replaced. Oh my god, you think out loud, "how much will it cost?" He comes up with a high-end estimate.

"By the way," he continues, "I know an excellent, very reliable furnace man who will give you a great price if you use my name. As a matter of fact, why don't I just call him for you?" If you go along with the scam, you have a new furnace (or water heater) before you know it. And you'll be lucky if it's new instead of rebuilt. And then he may clean up your old furnace and sell it to your neighbor.

Lesson: If a government or agency "official" comes to your door and wants access to your home, ask for his identification and his business card. Tell him to wait outside and then call the number. Check to see that he is legit. Even if he is, give him access only to the thing he is there to inspect. Do not take him up on any offer to get you a special price on a repair or replacement. If he makes such an offer, report it to the government agency. And don't hire professionals without checking references first.

In short, follow the guidelines laid out in Chapters 1 and 2. Don't give in to temptation when you hear about an emergency that a stranger has uncovered just in time or because someone wants to give you a today-only bargain.

Nightmare Alley

Following are some stories of folks who hired contractors and who entered "The Twilight Zone" as a result of bad work by dishonest "professionals." I appeared on one "Home" show episode that was dedicated to home repair and remodeling scams. As part of an of-necessity brief segment, we superficially covered what homeowners could do to protect themselves from contractor scams.

The Shark and the Sharkeys

Eddie and Ruby Sharkey of Memphis, Tennessee, appeared with me on the show, along with Tennessee state representative David Shirley. The Sharkeys had wanted to add a den and bathroom to their home and to expand their bedroom. They called a contractor who was running a heavy ad campaign in the Memphis area. He gave them an estimate for the job as well as several references regarding other work he had done. The

Sharkeys checked out the other projects and were impressed with the remodeler's work. They even checked him out with the local home remodelers' association and the Better Business Bureau. They agreed on a price of approximately $16,000 and signed a contract. The Sharkeys paid $12,000 up front.

The contractor's crew showed up on time and proceeded to rip out one end of the Sharkeys' home. They paid him the balance. But when the building crew failed to show up when due, Eddie called the contractor, who apologized for being tardy but said that his crew had gotten stuck finishing another job. The same thing happened the next day. After several days went by with the end of their home left open and their pavement partially demolished, Eddie decided to look into the contractor's business dealings. He did a little private-eye work and discovered that there were other homeowners who were in the same straits—lots of them!

Ruby and Eddie organized a group of these victims. In the meantime, they received notices of mechanics' liens. That's right, the remodeler hadn't been paying his bills from suppliers and subs. And many of the other victims found themselves in the same predicament. Their homes were in disarray. They were out substantial sums of money. They owed bills to suppliers and subs. And they still needed work to be done to rectify the conditions of their homes and their lives.

The victims' group went to the legal authorities and pressed charges against the contractor. And believe it or not, the guy received a jail sentence. But this didn't directly help Ruby and Eddie or their friends. The Sharkeys had to lay out an additional $16,000 by the time the entire job was properly finished. A total of $32,000 and one full year were spent in finalizing the complete renovation.

What did the Sharkeys do *right*? They checked the contractor's references. They went to the BBB and checked him out with the local home remodelers' association. So what went wrong? No one had complained to the consumer agencies, so there was no way to determine if the business in question had done anything wrong. Therefore, the remodelers' association and the BBB had no records of complaints against the remodeler. The Sharkeys didn't use references as a *source* of finding a contractor. They didn't check out the contractor's reputation with his suppliers.

They also made the mistake of paying a large sum of money up front. And they didn't insist on a completion bond and/or joint control.

Update: On the day of our "Home" appearance, Representative

Shirley was almost nine years into his effort to get the Tennessee legislature to do away with mechanics' liens. Because of a dishonest contractor, he himself had once been victimized by mechanics' liens. The reason for his passion about this issue—and I completely agree with it— is that suppliers and subcontractors should have no dealings beyond the people with whom they do business. If they do business with contractors who don't pay their bills, their recourse should be to go after the contractor.

Another way to look at it is like this. If you buy a Zenith TV set from April's Appliances and April fails to pay Zenith for it, Zenith has no right to come to your home and demand the payment that April failed to pay Zenith. The same is true for any other business transaction. Why should suppliers and subs have that right? Your deal is with the contractor. The contractor's deal is with his or her suppliers and subs.

It took David Shirley ten years to get the bill passed in the face of stiff opposition from the building suppliers' lobby in Tennessee. If you would like the same thing accomplished in your state, write to your state senator and assemblyperson (or representative).

The Multiple Breakdown

Here is a story that was told to me by Teddi Kessie, a woman who operates a contractor-referral service in Los Angeles. She had referred a particular general contractor for several years with excellent feedback from her clients. One time she referred him to an older couple to do several jobs, including the installation of a new roof. Several days into the job, the couple called Teddi and asked her to come over and look at what had happened. Evidently the contractor had endeavored to do the labor on the roof by himself, instead of subbing the work out. Without going into details about the job, it seems that the contractor became dysfunctional during the work. It rained a lot that winter, and no sooner would he correct one part of the problem than another place on the roof would spring a leak. And then there wasn't enough of a slope on the rebuilt roof, so water was puddling instead of running off. The job was a mess, and then the contractor disappeared. No one could reach him—no matter how hard they tried.

The homeowners were distraught, and the wife was in fear that her husband, who was frail to begin with, would have a heart attack. Teddi, being a caring and responsible person, felt bad that her clients were so distressed. She mulled over the situation and decided to call another contractor and pay him for the corrective work. This integrity cost her $7,000.

Lesson: Keep in mind that the contractor was licensed and bonded. So what went wrong that couldn't be rectified? First of all, the homeowners and the referral service did not note which company issued the completion bond. Nor did they check to see if the bond was current before they signed the contract. Had the homeowners or Teddi been diligent enough, they could have tried to get the California Contractors' State License Board to follow up on the case, and they could have sued.

The Case of the Liening Windows

Pete and Pat (really) hired an architect to redesign their kitchen. In addition to the kitchen, they wanted to have a wall moved and a bathroom added onto the house. The architect recommended a contractor—I'll call him Perry—who worked under two different licenses. One license was held by a partnership, in which Perry was a partner, that limited itself exclusively to commercial building and remodeling. The other license was held exclusively by Perry.

The contract was made with Perry's own contracting firm. The work was going along fine when, one day, Pat received a statement from the window supplier. The statement required Pat to sign a note saying that she would be responsible for payment for the new windows in the event that the contractor named in the statement failed to pay its bills. Pat signed the statement and returned it to the supplier. The contractor named on the statement was the *partnership* that Perry belonged to. It later turned out that several obligations that Perry made with creditors were done in the name of his commercial contracting partnership.

You may have figured it out by now. Perry was running short on cash. So instead of obtaining credit from his suppliers in his own name, he put it in the name of his partnership without his partners knowing about it. When he couldn't meet his debts, he let some of them default. And sure enough, the window supplier informed Pat and Pete that it was putting a lien on their home.

Understand that Pat and Pete are very particular people. They pride themselves on being responsible, paying their debts on time, and having squeaky-clean credit records. They did not take this lightly. They had checked to see that Perry was properly licensed and bonded and had relied on the architect's recommendation. They were as mad as hell and they weren't going to take it any more. They had their attorney threaten to sue not only Perry but also his partnership because it was the party that ordered the windows. Remember, Pat, in essence, had co-signed for the debt to the supplier. It took a while, but everything got straightened out: The partnership and Perry took care of the bills.

Lesson: Pat should not have signed for the windows. The purchase of the windows was between the contractor and the supplier. Even in Tennessee, where mechanics' liens are virtually outlawed, the supplier would have had the right to place a lien on Pete and Pat's place because Pat had personally co-signed for the windows. Also, Pete and Pat should not have relied exclusively upon the architect's recommendation. They should have checked out the contractor's record with the Better Business Bureau, the contractor regulatory agency (this episode occurred in a regulating state), and with recent customers.

The House with No Visible Means of Support

Larry and Annette hired an architect to add a second story to their home. The architect came highly recommended by a lawyer colleague of Annette's. They talked to the architect and liked him. Then they looked at some of the architect's finished designs and were duly impressed.

When the design work was finished, the architect recommended a contractor with whom he had worked previously. The contractor was hired based upon the architect's recommendation. The work seemed to go along fine, and payments were made according to schedule. After a while, Larry and Annette began to notice that little things didn't seem to fit right. So they had an inspection done by an engineer. He looked under the house and noticed that although new footings had been installed in the ground to support the extra weight of the addition, no part of the house was resting on the footings. In fact, the footings weren't placed where the house *could* rest upon them.

This meant that although the house had gained considerable weight, there were no additional load-bearing members under the house to support it. Larry and Annette withheld final payment, fired the contractor, and ended up dishing out an *extra* $30,000 in expenses to a contractor in order to rectify the situation. With the aid of an engineer, the new contractor came up with a solution. They jacked up the entire house and under it slid a steel bridge that rests upon the footings and upon which the house sits.

What might have caused such a dismal failure after the architect had recommended the contractor so highly? Larry and Annette later did some detective work and learned that the architect was in debt to the contractor for $50,000. Sound like a conflict of interest? I think so.

Lesson: By relying only upon the architect for a referral, our heroes depended solely upon an architect whom they had not known before this job. He was using their job to pay off a debt. Here is what they failed to do:

- ☑ Check the contractor's license. He didn't have one.
- ☑ Check the contractor's references.
- ☑ Insist on a completion bond to cover the full cost of the job.
- ☑ Talk to the building inspectors. It is now Larry's belief that the inspector never set foot onto the job site. He believes that the contractor headed off the inspector and made some special "arrangement" with him without the inspector ever getting out of his car.

I wish that Annette and Larry had followed up with a complaint to the BBB against both the architect and the contractor. I wish they had sued both of them as well and had reported the architect to the American Institute of Architects. Larry's attitude was that he did not want to go through the time, the effort, the frustration, and the negativity of going after the wrongdoers. I feel that if you don't bring justice against the bad guys, you encourage them to do it to someone else.

The Never-ending Nightmare

Andy and Marcia decided to add a second story to their house. They came upon a company that sells and installs prefabricated housing additions. They received a very low bid and decided to seek financing through a lender recommended by the contractor. However, the contractor's sales rep suddenly stopped returning their calls. It was just about the time that he learned that Andy was a lawyer. Andy feels that the return calls ceased because the bid was too low to be realistic and that the contractor wanted to avoid legal troubles once the job started and the contractor could start jacking up the price.

Not to be discouraged, Andy and Marcia decided to approach the project again through an architect. Marcia's cousin was an architect. Unfortunately, he had very little experience with residential second-story additions. He was given an ample budget of $150,000. (In many parts of the United States that would be enough to buy an acre of land and build a small mansion on it—but this took place in L.A.) After the quite elaborate plans were completed, Andy and Marcia couldn't find a contractor who was willing to do the job for that price.

However, they did find a contractor—whom I will refer to as I. M. Gonn—who was willing to redesign the plans and bring the job in for $150,000. As a matter of fact, they liked his design much better. They then found a savings and loan association that was willing to fund the loan, providing that it could disperse the funds through its own funding control department (see Chapter 2 and the Glossary). However, the federal banking regulators decided that the lender's loan program was too risky and stopped it before the loan could be funded.

By this time Marcia and Andy were ready to tear their hair out. So they sat down with Gonn and worked out a way to reduce the cost of the project by doing away with some of the less cost-effective amenities. Actually, they discarded the idea of a second story and decided to add on to the ground floor. They found a bank that was willing to finance, but Gonn's partner was insistent that they use a joint control company that he recommended. When the bank insisted on using its own funding control company, the contractor backed out of the deal. Strange behavior? You bet.

After thinking it over, the contractor came back and agreed to do the job with the bank's funding control. Marcia and Andy moved out of the house for seven months so that the remodeling could progress without their being in the middle of the havoc. The work started, and the first thing to go was the old roof. The open roof, however, was not tarped properly, and one night the rain got in and destroyed a portion of the ceilings below. The contractor pledged that he would make good on the ceilings and proceeded to bring in extra drywall for that purpose. The contractor had started work on framing, rough plumbing and electrical, windows, insulation, and stucco. As various parts of the house were being drywalled, the contractor went bankrupt. Evidently he was not managing his business well and was unable to fund the various projects he was working on. At this point Andy and Marcia were on the brink of bankruptcy themselves. They were paying rent on an apartment, a mortgage, and a second mortgage that was financing the remodeling. Their savings had run out. But just in the nick of time, Andy received a $40,000 inheritance from his late grandmother. (It's a good thing he treated her right while she was living.)

Shortly after that, Andy and Marcia discovered that Gonn's partner held an interest in the joint control company that he had originally insisted they use. Thankfully, Andy and Marcia had avoided using that joint control company. Can you imagine what might have happened to their money if they had put it in Gonn's partner's funding company? Fortunately, they hadn't lost any money because the funds were still in the hands of their legitimate joint control company.

Andy approached the heating, air-conditioning, electrical, and plumbing subcontractors who had been working for I. M. Gonn. They agreed to work for Andy and Marcia. Around the corner from their home, Andy and Marcia saw a house being remodeled by a contractor named Willie Werk. The job seemed to be going along smoothly. They asked the owner what she thought of the general contractor. She was very pleased. In spite of the fact that the contractor wasn't licensed, they decided to hire him on the basis of their neighbor's recommendation. They made a time-and-materials contract with him. This meant that they would pay him for the materials he purchased and for his labor based upon the number of hours worked on the job.

This worked well. Willie got along fine with the subs whom Andy and Marcia had hired, and the work progressed smoothly. In three weeks Willie got the house into livable shape. But . . . when the contractor was a couple of weeks from finishing, the work suddenly slowed down dramatically. It seemed never to end as the labor costs kept accumulating at a rate of $5,000 per week. Our heroes had no choice but to fire Willie Werk.

They then set about finding specialty contractors to finish the job. They looked for painters, carpenters, a drywall installer, and a hardwood-floor installer. A floor man recommended by a supplier proved to be excellent. A tile supplier recommended a tiler who proved to be incompetent. The work was poor and wasn't done on time. When Marcia told him that his services would no longer be required, he demanded payment for a complete job. She refused. He gave her an alternative. He wanted her to go on a date with him! Marcia responded, "I am going to give you $500. Then you are going to leave. Because when my husband gets home I am going to tell him what you said. And if you are still here, he will kill you."

Marcia's parents' friends recommended a painter (whom can you trust, if not your parents' friends?) He signed an agreement with Marcia and Andy and furnished them with a contractor's license number. The job was to cost $3,850, including an advance payment of $350. This left a balance of $3,500. The painter was an elderly Romanian man who showed up for the job with another elderly gentleman to assist him. They worked well but slowly. After three weeks the job was only two-thirds complete. And some of it needed to be redone. The painters insisted that they needed more money. They wanted the balance of $3,500 before they would continue with the work. Andy offered $2,200, which would cover almost two-thirds of the $3,850 total. An argument ensued, and the painters refused to leave.

Marcia and Andy had to call the security patrol service to which they subscribed. Only upon the arrival of the security guards did the painters leave. If you think that this is bizarre enough for you, hold on to your paintbrush. Andy and Marcia began receiving hostile and threatening phone calls from people with Romanian accents.

Finally, a woman who identified herself as the assistant painter's daughter-in-law told Andy that there were ways other than money by which one could extract payment. She mentioned the vulnerability of one's wife, children, and home. Who knows, a fire could accidentally occur.

Our heroes went to the police, claimed that they were victims of extortion and assault, and filed a criminal complaint. The city attorney held a hearing and warned the painter's family to cease its intimidating tactics.

The painters sued in small claims court. They asked for the balance owed of $3,500. The judge heard the story and awarded the painters $1,950, bringing their total to $2,300. Andy and Marcia are now suing the painters and their families for the harassment inflicted upon them and for the work that had to be redone.

The outcome? Our couple moved into the unfinished house. They hired a licensed painter to finish the paint job and to finish the drywall and carpentry work as well—it's as if they never learned. Fortunately, the work was finished satisfactorily. But it took another six months. They did not lose much money through all of this, but imagine the hassles and delays.

In the Introduction to this book I mentioned what a hell it could be if a contracting job went awry. Now you know.

Lesson: In addition to a funding control company, Andy and Marcia should have sought a contractor who could provide a completion bond. In this case, they later learned, the contractor was in financial trouble and could not have acquired such a bond. This would have been a dead giveaway that the contractor would have been a risk. They were lucky that their bank did not allow the joint control to go to a company that the contractor *insisted* upon.

Their next mistake was to use a nonlicensed contractor on a time-

and-materials basis. Too risky. The time factor encourages the contractor to work slowly.

The elderly painter offered a license number, but later, when Andy and Marcia checked out the license, they learned that it belonged to a friend of the painter. Andy and Marcia never did find out if the painters were really professionals. Maybe that's why they were so slow. Now I want you to determine what efforts Andy and Marcia should have taken to assure a better chance at smooth sailing. Laziness is often the reason that many folks don't make the extra effort to double-check their contractors. And they often pay for it in the end with a lot more work. I do it myself on occasion. Shame on all of us.

Bobbi and Bobby and the Double Whammy

Several years ago Bobbi and Bobby were looking for a contractor to remodel their bathroom and to build a walk-in closet. Bobbi had a friend at work named Brenda. Brenda's boyfriend, Brent, with whom she lived, happened to be a contractor. Brent gave a $12,000 estimate for the job. Bobby asked for proof of a bond and for Brent's license number. Brent said that he would get the number from his partner and would bring a copy of the bond as well. He asked for 30 percent of the price up front. Bobbi and Bobby paid it.

Bobbi picked out the faucets, a whirlpool tub, the tiles, and the fixtures. The work started, and Bobbi asked for the license number and bond again. Brent had forgotten them. The workers started showing up only intermittently, sometimes with gaps of a few weeks. Then suddenly the work picked up again, and Brent said that he needed another payment because he was actually just getting back into the business full swing and the funds were running out. Bobbi and Bobby didn't see the red flag—and if *you* don't see it in this scenario, you're color blind. Apparently Brent was either outright swindling them or was using their funds to finance other jobs.

So they paid again. Soon after, Bobbi learned that Brenda was going on a vacation to the Caribbean. And then the remodeling stopped.

Then it dawned on Bobbi that her money was being used to finance Brent and Brenda's Caribbean wingding. Brent and his workers never showed up again. There was no partner, no license, no bond, and no California address for Brent. Brenda then claimed that she and Brent had broken up and that she had no idea where he'd gone. Bobby and Bobbi were out $9,000. Oh, yeah, Brent hadn't paid for the fixtures, either. So they still had to cough up for that bill as well. They ended up having to pay an additional $15,000 to get their bathroom redone.

Lesson: Are you kidding? By now you should be able to write a book of your own on what Bobbi and Bobby did wrong. But look, there's more!

Bobbi Part II

It is now several years later. Bobbi has remarried (the divorce had nothing to do with the bathroom debacle). New house. New hubby. Bobbi and Robert decide to add ten feet to their bedroom and to remodel the bathroom (oh, no—not again!). I'm going to give it to you in a nutshell. The contractor came recommended from a friend. The contract was for $25,000. They didn't check him out with suppliers, references, the BBB, the state licensing authority, or the workmen's compensation insurer. They didn't look at his previous or ongoing work. No joint control, no lien releases . . . nothin'. Yes, I know what you're thinking: "Doesn't this woman ever learn?"

The contractor asked for, and received, 25 percent as a deposit (illegal in California) and 25 percent when he began installing the structural framework. Which means that he could get $12,500 just a few days into the job. A few days after the framing started, he became hard to find. Robert would call and leave messages, which the contractor soon stopped returning. And they kept giving him the benefit of the doubt— he seemed like such a nice guy.

The dumpster outside was filled with debris from the demolition part of the job. The portable toilet (where do the workmen wash their hands after they make use of those things? Yecch) was sitting on the property. Then the suppliers started sending lien notices for lumber and fixtures.

Robert told the dumpster guy that he bore no responsibility and that the trash collector would have to take the issue up with the contractor. So the trash hauler showed up, dumped the load from the dumpster onto Bobbi and Robert's lawn, and drove off. The portable toilet was taken away (thank heavens), and liens were placed on the property.

Bobbi and Robert had to pay the hauler to come back and take the debris away so that their replacement contractor could have clear access to their property. Their lawyer wrote to the original contractor and formally requested return of payments. The letter also told the contractor that his services were no longer required. Robert then called two of the contractor's suppliers about what the contractor had done. The next time he called the contractor, Robert *told* him that he was fired and that he would do whatever he could to get his money back. The contractor became irate and told Robert that he had no right to bad-mouth him to his suppliers. (This is what is known in Yiddish as *chutzpah*.)

As of this writing, Robert and Bobbi have filed a complaint with the California Contractors' State License Board and are in the midst of filing complaints with the BBB, the city attorney's office, and the suppliers who had been dealing with the contractor. They are also considering filing a civil suit in superior court.

Lesson: It is easier to go through the tedious process of checking out a contractor's history, credentials, and business practices than it is to reap the consequences of dealing with a bum.

Rosemary and Sage: They Just Didn't Have the Thyme

I will abbreviate this story because it gets too depressing and complicated. Rosemary—who lives with her son, Sage, decided to have a tree removed from the side of her house. Literally *from* the side of her house. As it had grown over the years, it was pushing against the house and warping it. This process left a corner of the house with no visible means of support.

About a year later, she noticed that the house was sinking in another area. It turned out that a part of the structure was not supported by a foundation. There was just a mudsill (wood resting on earth). Rosemary got estimates from several contractors, and they were high. She knew that a member of her church who taught Sunday school was a contractor. She asked other church members for references, and they said that they liked Joe's work.

Rosemary had Joe look the problem over and told him what the other contractors had bid (a big, *Big*, *Big* mistake). He underbid them and was hired. He gave her a one-page contract. She paid him a third of the price. And he started the job.

She checked out his license. She asked for permits to be "pulled" for the job. Then she determined—based upon Joe's saying so—that permits were not required for repairing an existing foundation.

He didn't show up on a regular basis to supervise his workers. The job didn't go well. Some days the men didn't show at all. Rosemary was losing patience. When she asked questions, she couldn't get a decent response. All of her under-house pipes were exposed, and winter was setting in. She demanded results.

Joe fired his men and took over the work himself. He demanded another third of the money. Rosemary paid it. But the work dragged on. And it didn't look right. An argument ensued when Rosemary asked Joe why his work was so slow and so poor. Joe said that if she were a man he would have punched her. So much for church kinship. He quit. She fired him.

The snow came. The pipes froze and cracked. Rosemary paid $650 to plumbers. She hired another contractor. He told her that the new foundation, which should have had its footing buried eighteen inches into the ground, was resting about two inches deep. The part that was resting where the tree roots had been was sitting on broken pieces of old foundation that had been covered by dirt. There was no solid new footing below that spot. The house was doomed to sink.

This time Rosemary was determined to do things right. She got a detailed contract complete with drawings and specs. It was $2,000 more expensive than the first job—mainly because much of the old work would have to be undone. I have since advised her how to go after Joe's $5,000 California bond. I have also told her how to pursue him in small claims court.

Lesson: A church is a church. A synagogue is a synagogue. A mosque is a mosque. And business is business. Trust anyone you want. But only after you have a *detailed* contract. And check out that liability bond. Get a completion bond. Don't pay for work that hasn't been done. And if you don't know—as my Dad used to say—your ass from your elbow, don't allow structural work to go on without the supervision of an engineer, architect, or building inspector. *Someone* should have been overseeing this work. Even honest contractors may not know all there is to know about renovation if their own companies are doing all of the work.

Appendix A

State Contractor Regulatory Agencies and Licensing Laws

Be sure that your contractor has agreed in writing to provide an adequate amount of coverage in a completion bond—regardless of what state law may, or may not, require. Workmen's compensation insurance should also be adequate, regardless of state requirements. Ask to see a copy of the bond and insurance policy and then check with the issuing companies to see that the coverages are valid.

In states that have no licensing requirements, check to see what regulations may exist in your county or municipality and make sure that your contractor complies.

Alabama

Alabama's licensing procedures do not apply to single family homes and townhouses, except for swimming pool contractors. Subcontractors do not have to be licensed. Other contractors need to be licensed only for jobs whose cost exceeds $20,000. Licenses are issued in six different maximum-bid categories. Check to see that your contractor is not bidding for a job too costly for his or her license. Licenses expire on December 31. Be sure that your contractor's license is current.

Requirements
Licensing Examination: No
Bond: No
Workmen's Compensation: No
Liability Insurance: No

State Licensing Board for General Contractors
125 South Ripley Street
Montgomery, AL 36130
(205) 261–2839

Alaska

All contractors must be licensed. They must also possess a state business license. Plumbing and electrical contractors must possess a Certificate of Fitness from the Department of Labor.

Requirements
Licensing Examination: Yes—for general contractors, electricians, plumbers, refrigeration, heating and air-conditioning contractors, and some others (contact regulators)
Bond: Yes
Workmen's Compensation: Yes
Liability Insurance: Yes

Department of Commerce and Economic Development
Division of Occupational Licensing
P.O. Box D
Juneau, AK 99811–0800
(907) 465–2546

Arizona

All home improvement and repair contractors must be licensed.

Requirements
License Examination: Yes
Bond: Yes—$75,000 or contribution to state recovery fund
Workmen's Compensation: No
Liability Insurance: No

Registrar of Contracts
800 West Washington, 6th Floor
Phoenix, AZ 85007
(602) 542–1525

Arkansas

No state requirement for residential remodelers, though municipalities may require such registration with the state (check with your local government). Nonresidential contractors whose projects cost more than $20,000 must be licensed. Registrations expire November 30. Licenses expire annually.

Requirements
Licensing Examination: No (except for nonresidential contractors)
Bond: No
Workmen's Compensation: No
Liability Insurance: Yes

Contractors Licensing Board
621 East Capitol Avenue
Little Rock, AR 72202
(501) 372–4661

California

All contractors who build or repair structures. Licenses must be renewed every two years.

Requirements
Licensing Examination: Yes
Bond: Yes
Workmen's Compensation: Yes
Liability Insurance: No

Contractors State License Board
P.O. Box 26000
3132 Bradshaw Street
Sacramento, CA 95826
In CA: (800) 321–2752 / (916) 366–5153

Colorado

No regulation of contractors. (Booooo!) The Colorado State Board on Electrical and Plumbing is the exception. Call (303) 894–2300.

Connecticut

Virtually all contractors and subcontractors must be licensed. Licenses expire annually according to a chart issued by the state.

Requirements
License Examination: No
Bond: No
Workmen's Compensation: Yes
Liability Insurance: Yes

Commissioner of Consumer Protection
Department of Occupational Licensing
State Office Building
165 Capital Avenue
Hartford, CT 06106
(203) 566–3386

Delaware

All contractors must obtain a license, register with the state Department of Labor, and supply proof of workmen's comp. All licenses must be renewed annually by December 31.

Requirements
Licensing Examination: No
Bond: No (except for nonresident contractors, who must post a bond equal to 6 percent of the cost of the job)
Workmen's Compensation: Yes
Liability Insurance: Yes

Department of Finance
Division of Revenue
Carvel State Building
820 North French Street
Wilmington, DE 19801
(302) 571–3369

District of Columbia

All contractors who charge more than $300 for a job must have licenses.

Requirements
Licensing Examination: No
Bond: Yes (but limited)
Workmen's Compensation: No
Liability: Yes

Department of Consumer and Regulatory Affairs
614 H Street, N.W., Suite 1120
Washington, DC 20001
(202) 727–7089

Florida

All contractors must be licensed. Licenses must be renewed by June 30, every two years.

Requirements

Licensing Examination: Yes
Bond: No
Workmen's Compensation: No
Liability Insurance: Yes

Department of Professional Regulation
The Construction Industry Licensing Board
P.O. Box 2
Jacksonville, FL 32201–0002
(904) 359–6310

Georgia

Out-of-state contractors must register for any jobs costing more than $10,000. Air-conditioning, electrical, utility, and plumbing contractors must be licensed by the Construction Industry Licensing Board.

Requirements

License Examination: No
Bond: Yes (required in the amount of 10 percent of each contract price)
Workmen's Compensation: Yes
Liability Insurance: No

State Revenue Commissioner
Contract Unit, Tax Division
Trinity-Washington Building
Atlanta, GA 30334
(404) 656-4080

Construction Industry Licensing Board
166 Pryor Street, S.W.
Atlanta, GA 30303–3465
(404) 656–2448

Hawaii

All contractors must be licensed, and all must deposit $150 into a Contractors Recovery Fund, which, upon court order, reimburses those injured by the actions of a contractor. Awards are limited to $12,500. License must be renewed by April 30 of even-numbered years.

Requirements
Licensing Examination: Yes
Bond: No (see above for Recovery Fund)
Workmen's Compensation: Yes
Liability Insurance: Yes

Department of Commerce and Consumer Affairs
Contractors License Board
P.O. Box 3469
Honolulu, HI 96801
(808) 548–4100

Idaho

No licensing of residential contractors. (Hissss!)

Illinois

No licensing of residential contractors. However, plumbing contractors are regulated through the Department of Public Health, Division of Environmental Health. Call (217) 782–5830.

Indiana

No statewide licensing of residential contractors. The exception is plumbers, who are regulated by the Professional Licensing Agency. Call (317) 232–2980.

Iowa

Only construction contractors must be registered with (not licensed by) the state.

Requirements
Licensing Examination: No
Bond: Yes—5 percent of cost of job or $1,000, whichever is greater
Workmen's Compensation: Yes
Liability Insurance: No

Department of Employment Services
Division of Labor
1000 East Grand Avenue
Des Moines, IA 50319–0209
(515) 281–3606

Kansas

No licensing requirements. Contractors and subcontractors must register for each job with the Department of Revenue.

Requirements
Licensing Examination: No
Bond: Yes, 8 percent of cost of job or $1,000, whichever is greater
Workmen's Compensation: No
Liability Insurance: No

Kentucky

No licensing requirements for construction or repair contractors. However, plumbers are regulated through the Department of Housing, Department of Plumbing, (502) 564–3580; and electricians are regulated through the State Fire Marshal, (502) 564–3626.

Louisiana

No licensing of contractors who build or work on home residences. (Hissss!)

Maine

No regulation of residential contractors. Plumbers and electricians are regulated through the Department of Professional and Financial Regulation, Division of Licensing and Enforcement, (207) 582–8723.

Maryland

This one gets complicated. All contractors must be licensed. All home improvement contractors must get an additional license for that specialty. All plumbing and electrical contractors must also get licenses from the State Board of Commissioners of Practical Plumbing and the Maryland Statewide Master Electrical Licensing Board (they evidently like cumbersome names in Maryland), respectively. Construction firm (contractor) licenses expire May 1. Home improvement contractor licenses expire June

30, in odd-numbered years. A Home Improvement Guarantee Fund compensates for actual losses due to wrong conduct by contractors.

Requirements
Licensing Examination: Yes
Bond: Must contribute to Guarantee Fund (see above)
Workmen's Compensation: Yes (or provide evidence of self-insurance)
Liability Insurance: No

All contractors
Comptroller of the Treasury
Retail Sales Tax Division
State License Bureau
301 West Preston Street
Baltimore, MD 21201–2383
(301) 225–1550

Home improvement contractors
Department of Licensing and Regulation
Home Improvement Commission
501 St. Paul Place, Room 801
Baltimore, MD 21202
(301) 333–6309

Massachusetts

All construction *supervisors* must be licensed for work on structures up to a maximum of 35,000 cubic feet. Licenses are issued initially for three years and must be renewed at two-year intervals.

Requirements
Licensing Examination: Yes
Bond: No
Workmen's Compensation: No
Liability Insurance: No

State Board of Building Regulations and Standards
John W. McCormack State Office Building
One Ashburton Place, Room 1301
Boston, MA 02108
(617) 727–3200

Michigan

All residential contractors must be licensed. Licenses must be renewed by every May 31.

Requirements
Licensing Examination: Yes
Bond: No, but contractor must contribute to lien recovery fund
Workmen's Compensation: No
Liability Insurance: No

Department of Licensing and Regulation
Residential Builders and Maintenance and Alteration Contractors Board
P.O. Box 30245
Lansing, MI 48909
(517) 373–0678

Minnesota

No licensing of residential contractors. Plumbing contractors are licensed through the State Health Department, (612) 296–3871; and electrical contractors are licensed through the Board of Electricity, (612) 642–0800.

Mississippi

No licensing of contractors is required. Certificates of Responsibility are required for projects costing more than $100,000.

Requirements
Licensing Examination: Yes (but only for conditions described above)
Bond: No
Workmen's Compensation: No
Liability Insurance: No

State Board of Contractors
2001 Airport Road #101
Jackson, MS 39208
(601) 354–6161

Missouri

No licensing of contractors. (Hissss!)

Montana

Except for plumbers and electrical contractors, no licensing of residential contractors.

Building Codes Bureau
Capitol Station
1218 East Sixth Avenue
Helena, MT 59620
(406) 444-3933

Nebraska

All contractors *and each individual contract* must be registered. Electricians are licensed through the State Electrical Division.

Requirements
Licensing Exam: No
Bond: 10 percent of contract price for first $100,000; 5 percent thereafter; $1,000 minimum; no bond required for jobs under $2,500
Workmen's Compensation: No
Liability Insurance: No

Nebraska Department of Revenue
P.O. Box 94818
Lincoln, NE 68509-4818
(402) 471-2971

Nevada

All contractors must be licensed. Licenses expire annually.

Requirements
Licensing Examination: Yes
Bond: Yes, but only for the first five years of licensing
Workmen's Compensation: Yes
Liability Insurance: No

State Contractor Boards
70 Linden Street
Reno, NV 89502
(702) 789-0141

1800 Industrial Road
Las Vegas, NV 89158
(702) 486–3500

New Hampshire

No licensing of residential contractors. Plumbers are licensed through the New Hampshire Plumbers Board, (603) 271–3267; and electricians are licensed through the New Hampshire Electricians Board, (603) 271–3748.

New Jersey

All residential contractors must be registered (not licensed). However, plumbers and electricians must be licensed through their respective licensing boards in the Department of Law and Public Safety, (201) 648–4010.

Requirements
Licensing Examination: No
Bond: No
Workmen's Compensation: Yes
Liability Insurance: Yes

Electricians and plumbers
Department of Law and Public Safety
Division of Consumer Affairs
1100 Raymond Boulevard, Room 504
Newark, NJ 07102
(201) 648–4010

Other contractors
Department of Banking
Division of Supervision
License Section
CN 040, 20 West State Street
Trenton, NJ 08625
(609) 292–5340 or 5341

New Mexico

All contractors must be licensed. Licenses expire every two years from the date of issue.

Requirements
Licensing Examination: Yes
Bond: Yes
Workmen's Compensation: Yes
Liability Insurance: No

Regulation and Licensing Department
Construction Industries Division
725 St. Michaels Drive
P.O. Box 25101
Sante Fe, NM 87504
(505) 827–7030

New York

No licensing of contractors. (Booooo!)

North Carolina

Licensing required only for contractors who perform jobs that cost $45,000 or more. Plumbing and electrical contractors are licensed by the Plumbing and Heating Board and the Electrical Board, respectively. Licenses expire every December 31.

Requirements
Licensing Examination: Yes
Bond: No
Workmen's Compensation: No
Liability Insurance: No

Licensing Board for General Contractors
P.O. Box 17187
Raleigh, NC 27619
(919) 781–8771

North Dakota

All contractors must be licensed. Licenses must be renewed every February 1.

Requirements
Licensing Examination: No
Bond: Yes (very small)

Workmen's Compensation: Yes
Liability Insurance: No

Secretary of State
State Capitol
600 East Boulevard Avenue
Bismarck, ND 58505–0500
(701) 224–2900

Ohio
No licensing regulations. (Booooo!)

Oklahoma
No licensing of contractors except for plumbers and electricians who are licensed by the Department of Health. Out-of-state contractors must be bonded and must notify the state Tax Commission—(405) 521–4437—and the assessor of the county in which the work is to be performed. This must be done before work starts and when it is completed.

Oregon
All contractors must be registered. Registration expires one year from the date of issuance. Plumbers and electricians must be licensed by the Building Codes Agency.

Requirements
Licensing Examination: No
Bond: Yes (varies)
Workmen's Compensation: Yes
Liability Insurance: Yes

Construction Contractors Board
700 Summer N.E., Suite 300
Salem, OR 93710–0151
(503) 378–4621

Pennsylvania
No licensing of contractors. (Hissss!)

Rhode Island

All contractors must be registered. Registrations expire one year from the date of issuance.

Requirements
Licensing Examination: No
Bond: No
Workmen's Compensation: Yes
Liability Insurance: Yes

Office of Professional Regulation
Department of Health
75 Davis Street
Providence, RI 02908
(401) 277–2827

South Carolina

General contractors who construct or improve any structure for more than $30,000 and residential builders and related subcontractors who construct or improve certain buildings for more than $5,000 must be licensed. Consult respective agencies for details. General contractors' licenses expire annually on January 1. Residential builders' licenses expire on June 30.

Requirements
Licensing Examination: Yes (requirements vary with specialties)
Bond: No
Workmen's Compensation: No
Liability Insurance: No

State of South Carolina Licensing Board for Contractors
1300 Pickens Street
P.O. Box 5737
Columbia, SC 29250
(803) 734–8954

South Carolina Residential Builders Commission
2221 Devine Street, Suite 530
Columbia, SC 29205
(803) 734–9174

South Dakota

No licensing of contractors. Plumbers are regulated through the State Plumbing Commission, (605) 773–3429.

Tennessee

Contractors are required to have a license if the contract is for $25,000 or more. In the four largest counties, home improvement contractors are required to obtain a license through a separate procedure. Licenses are not required when the construction of a dwelling for resale is on private property in the county of one's residence in counties with less than 60,000 population. General contractors' licenses expire annually on the last day of the twelfth month following issuance. Home improvement contractors' licenses expire annually on the date of issue.

Requirements

Licensing Examination: Yes
Bond: Only for home improvement contractors who do not submit financial statements or other surety
Workmen's Compensation: No
Liability Insurance: No

Tennessee Board for Licensing Contractors
500 James Robertson Parkway, Suite 110
Nashville, TN 37243–1150
(800) 544–7693/(615) 741–2121

Texas

No licensing of contractors except for those who provide "residential service contracts." These contracts include maintaining, repairing, and replacing structural components or the electrical, plumbing, heating, cooling, or air-conditioning systems of residential properties. Licenses are obtained from the Texas Real Estate Commission. Plumbers are licensed through the State Plumbing Commission, (512) 458–2145.

Utah

All contractors must be licensed. Licenses must be renewed by July 31 of each odd-numbered year.

Requirements

Licensing Examination: Yes
Bond: For jobs of $2,000 or more, if requested by client, for full amount of contract price

Workmen's Compensation: Yes
Liability Insurance: Yes

Department of Commerce
Division of Occupational and Professional Licensing
P.O. Box 45802
Salt Lake City, UT 84145
(801) 530–6628

Vermont

No licensing of contractors. Plumbers and electricians are regulated by the Department of Labor and Industry, (802) 828–2458.

Virginia

All contractors must obtain licenses. Licenses must be renewed every two years by the end of the month of original issuance.

Requirements
Licensing Examination: Yes
Bond: No
Workmen's Compensation: No
Liability Insurance: Yes

Department of Commerce
State Board of Contractors
3600 West Broad Street
Richmond, VA 23230
(800) 552–3016 (in VA)/(804) 257–8500

Washington

All contractors must be registered.

Requirements
Licensing Examination: No
Bond: Yes
Workmen's Compensation: No
Liability Insurance: Yes

Department of Labor and Industries
Contractors' Section
P.O. Box 9689
Olympia, WA 98504–9689
(206) 753–6807

West Virginia

No licensing of contractors. They must, however, have a business registration certificate. Electrical contractors must be licensed through the state fire commissioner. Out-of-state contractors must either deposit 6 percent of the contract fee in a Contractor's Use Tax Fund or post a surety bond to be approved by the tax commissioner.

Wisconsin

No licensing of contractors. Plumbers are licensed through the Department of Industry, Labor and Human Relations, Division of Safety and Building, (608) 266–3815.

Wyoming

No licensing of *resident* contractors. However, nonresident contractors—defined as those who have not continuously done business in the state for five years *or* who have less than $5,000 worth of real property in Wyoming prior to bidding on a contract—must be licensed. Workmen's Compensation and surety bonds are required only for nonresident, employer contractors.

Department of Employment
Division of Employment Affairs
Herschler Building
112 West 25th Street
Cheyenne, WY 82002
(307) 777–7261

Appendix B

Sample Contract and Payment Schedule

Following is an actual contract between a married couple and an incorporated contractor. It consists of the agreement—or contract—and separate specifications sheets and a payment schedule, which form integral parts of the contract. The first page of the agreement shows the start and completion dates. Page 153 includes all of the "boilerplate," which is preprinted on the form. Some of the preprinted information in the contract is applicable in California; note that each state's requirements vary.

An analysis follows the contract. I did not analyze all of the "Terms and Conditions" because much of it is self-explanatory. I have chosen to constructively criticize *select* clauses of the agreement itself and of the various groups of specifications. For example, I have selected one specification from the group identified as "Pull-Down Stairs." I will leave it to the reader to find other ways that the specifications could be spelled out more clearly *for the homeowners' benefit and protection.*

Let me assure you that in the job that was completed under this contract, the homeowners did very well because the contractor is highly professional and ethical and was determined to please his clients.

The names and address of the homeowners have been omitted for obvious reasons.

An additional note: Some changes were necessary as the job progressed. And because the homeowners trusted the contractor, they worked without change orders. I strongly advise against doing that, if for no other reason that without written instructions, communications can go awry.

Property Improvement Agreement

Notice that the contractor's address and license number are prominent. Because the home is a condominium townhouse, a contingency

238 REV. 9/90

PROPERTY IMPROVEMENT AGREEMENT

THIS DOCUMENT CONSISTING OF THIS AGREEMENT, PLANS AND SPECIFICATIONS, IF ANY, AND NOTICE OF CANCELLATION, ALL ATTACHED HERETO AND MADE A PART HEREOF, SHALL CONSTITUTE THE AGREEMENT

THIS AGREEMENT IS BETWEEN

CONTRACTOR/ SELLER/ BENEFICIARY	NAME **BY ROGER PERRON, INC.**			DATE Feb. 22, 1991
	ADDRESS 1441 GARDENA AVE.,	CITY GLENDALE,	STATE CA 91204	PHONE (818) 241-8869	LICENSE NO 416079

BUYER/ OWNER	NAME			
	RESIDENCE ADDRESS	CITY	STATE	RESIDENCE PHONE
	PLACE OF BUSINESS (If Any)	CITY	STATE	BUSINESS PHONE

Hereinafter called "Buyer", "Owner" and/or "Trustor" agrees to pay therefore the price hereinafter set forth upon the following terms and conditions.

CONSTRUCTION PROJECT

PROJECT ADDRESS – STREET   CITY   STATE – PROVINCE   ZIP CODE

See Specifications

Also known as Legal Description: Lot# _____ Tract# _____ Block# _____

Recorded in Book# _____ Page# _____ in the office of the County Recorder of _____
State of California.
DESCRIPTION OF PROJECT: CONTRACTOR WILL CONSTRUCT THE IMPROVEMENTS IN THIS AGREEMENT AND DESCRIBED GENERALLY AS FOLLOWS

See Specifications

This contract is contingent upon approval from the condominium

Design Review Board.

☒ Check here if this space is insufficient for complete specifications (staple additions to original and each copy).
☐ Check here if there are plans (staple plans to original and each copy).
If checked, additional specifications or plans are attached to and incorporated in this Agreement.
NOT INCLUDED: THE FOLLOWING ITEMS ARE SPECIFICALLY EXCLUDED FROM THIS CONTRACT AND ARE TO BE PROVIDED BY THE OWNER

See Specifications

ALLOWANCES: The following items, where specific prices are indicated, are included in the Contract Price as allowances for the purchase price of those items to be selected by Owner. Owner and Contractor agree to adjust the Contract Price after verification of actual cost difference (if any) of said items selected by Owner.

See Specifications

APPLIANCES $ _____ *	LIGHT FIXTURES $ _____ *	BATH ACCESSORIES $ _____ *
FLOOR COVERING $ _____ *	HARDWARE FINISH $ _____ *	AND "OTHER" $ _____ *

Finish hardware is interpreted to include all knobs, pulls, hinges, catches, locks, drawer slides, accessories or other items that are normally installed subsequent to final painting. Light fixtures are interpreted to include only those fixtures that are surface mounted. Bath accessories are interpreted to include medicine cabinets, towel bars, paper holders, soap dishes, etc.

TIME FOR STARTING AND COMPLETING PROJECT: Work shall commence within ten days after the last to occur of the following: (1) Receipt by the Contractor of all necessary building permits; (2) Owner has complied with all Terms and Conditions of the Agreement to date; (3) Receipt of all construction funds by Escrow or Funding Control (if any). Subject to adjustment for the above

conditions, work shall begin approximately on March 8, 1991 and be substantially completed approximately on within six weeks with additional time to be allowed as detailed in paragraph entitled "Delays" of the Terms and Conditions on the back hereof. Commencement of work shall be defined as

(BRIEFLY DESCRIBE TYPE OF WORK REPRESENTING COMMENCEMENT)
Contractors failure to substantially commence work, without lawful excuse, within twenty (20) days from the date specified above is a violation of the Contractors License Law

CONTRACT PRICE

PAYMENT: Owner agrees to pay Contractor a total cash price of $ 19,375 OWNER represents that this agreement is a cash transaction where in no financing is contemplated and contractor acts in reliance on said representation.
The payment schedule will be

(1) Down payment of $ _____ (2) Payment schedule as follows: See Payment Schedule

All payments will be made within five (5) days after billing. Overdue payments will bear interest at the maximum legally permissible rate. If any payment is not made when due. Contractor may keep the job idle until such time as all payments due have been made. A failure of payment for a period in excess of said (5) days from the date specified above is to be considered a major breach

Contractor or Owner prior to commencement of construction and subject to lending institution (if any) approval, may request funds to be placed in an Escrow or Funding Voucher Control Service prior to commencement of work with funds to be disbursed to Contractor in accordance with the escrow instructions or voucher orders signed by the Contractor. In the absence of an Escrow or Funding Control Service, funds will be paid directly to the Contractor in accordance with the progress payments schedule referred to above.

NOTICE TO THE BUYER: (1) Do not sign this agreement before you read it or if it contains any blank spaces. (2) You are entitled to a completely filled in copy of this agreement. Owner acknowledges that he has read and received a legible copy of this agreement signed by Contractor, including all terms and conditions on the reverse side, before any work was done, and that he has read and received a legible copy of every document that owner has signed during the negotiation. If owner cancels this agreement after the right of recission has expired, and before commencement of construction, he shall pay Contractor the amount of expenses incurred to that date plus loss of profits.

TERMS AND CONDITIONS

The terms and conditions on the reverse side are expressly incorporated into this Agreement. This Agreement constitutes the entire understanding of the parties. No other understanding or representations, verbal or otherwise, shall be binding unless in writing and signed by both parties. This Agreement shall not become effective or binding upon Contractor until signed by Contractor or a principal of Contractor. By his signature below, Owner acknowledges receipt of a fully completed copy of this Agreement

NOTICE

Contractors are required by law to be licensed and regulated by the Contractors' State License Board. Any questions concerning a contractor may be referred to the Registrar Contractor's State License Board, 9835 Goethe Road, Sacramento, California 95827. Mailing address: P.O. Box 26000, Sacramento, California 95826.

You, as Owner or Tenant, have the right to require the Contractor to have a Performance and Payment Bond.

You, the buyer, may cancel this transaction at any time prior to midnight of the third business day after the date of this transaction. See the attached notice of cancellation form for an explanation of this right.

SALESMAN	REGISTRATION#	OWNER – BUYER SIGNATURE ✗	DATE 2/22/91
ACCEPTED BY CONTRACTOR – SELLER SIGNATURE ✗ Roger Perron		OWNER – BUYER SIGNATURE ✗	DATE 2/22/91

TERMS AND CONDITIONS

ASBESTOS/HAZARDOUS MATERIALS

1. Owner represents that the property being remodelled does not contain asbestos and/or other hazardous materials. This contract does not contemplate the removal of, testing for, disturbance, or disposal of asbestos, asbestos material, or other hazardous substances. If such items are found, contractor may cease work and request additional compensation from owner for appropriate corrective work and any other additional expenses incurred by the corrective work.

CONTRACTOR'S RIGHTS AND RESPONSIBILITIES

CONTRACTOR'S RIGHTS

1. SUBCONTRACTORS. Contractor may subcontract all or any portion of the work.

2. Contractor shall have the right to stop work and keep the job idle if payments are not made to him when due. Failure to make payment within five (5) days of the date that payment is due will be considered a material breach of this agreement. If the work shall be stopped for any reason, for a period of sixty (60) days, then Contractor may, at Contractor's option, upon five (5) days written notice, demand and receive payment for all work executed and material ordered or supplied and any other loss sustained, including Contractor's usual fee for overhead and profit based upon the contract price. Thereafter, Contractor is relieved from any further liability. In the event of work stoppage for any reason, Owner shall provide for protection of and be responsible for, any damage, warpage, racking or loss of material on the premises.

3. Contractor, at Contractor's option, may alter specifications only so as to comply with requirements of Governmental Agencies having jurisdiction over same. Any alteration or work undertaken to further this end shall be treated as an Extra Work.

CONTRACTOR'S RESPONSIBILITIES AND LIMITED WARRANTY

1. Contractor agrees to furnish the materials for the project and complete the work in a workmanlike manner. All materials furnished under this Agreement shall be construction grade and meet industry standards. Where brand names have been specified, Contractor may, at his option, select substitutes when such substitutions are due to unavailability or other circumstances beyond Contractor's control. All substitutions shall be consistent in quality and character to the selections previously specified. THE LIABILITY OF THE CONTRACTOR FOR DEFECTIVE MATERIALS OR INSTALLATION IS HEREBY LIMITED TO THE REPLACEMENT OR CORRECTION OF SAID DEFECTIVE MATERIAL AND OR INSTALLATION, AND NO OTHER CLAIMS OR DEMANDS WHATSOEVER SHALL BE MADE UPON OR ALLOWED AGAINST THE CONTRACTOR. THIS LIMITED WARRANTY EXTENDS ONLY TO OWNER AND IS NOT TRANSFERABLE. THERE IS NO IMPLIED WARRANTY OF MERCHANTABILITY NOR ANY IMPLIED WARRANTY OF FITNESS FOR ANY PARTICULAR PURPOSE. THERE ARE NO WARRANTIES EITHER EXPRESSED OR IMPLIED WHICH EXTEND BEYOND THE DESCRIPTION WITHIN THIS PARAGRAPH #1. THIS WARRANTY SHALL TERMINATE ONE YEAR FROM FINAL BUILDING INSPECTION OR THE DATE OF THE COMPLETION, WHICHEVER IS FIRST.

NOTE THAT EQUIPMENT, ASSEMBLIES, OR UNITS PURCHASED BY CONTRACTOR INCLUDED IN THIS CONTRACT ARE SOLD AND INSTALLED SUBJECT TO THE MANUFACTURER'S OR PROCESSOR'S GUARANTEE OR WARRANTIES, AND NOT CONTRACTOR'S. TO THE EXTENT PERMITTED BY APPLICABLE LAW, ALL WARRANTIES GIVEN BY MANUFACTURERS PERTAINING TO MATERIALS USED BY CONTRACTOR IN CONNECTION WITH THE PROJECT WILL BE PASSED THROUGH AND INURE TO THE BENEFIT OF OWNER.

2. Contractor shall pay all subcontractors, labors and material suppliers. Contractor shall, to the best of his ability, keep Owner's property free of valid labor or materialmen's liens.

ITEMS NOT RESPONSIBILITY OF CONTRACTOR

1. EXISTING VIOLATIONS AND CONDITIONS. Contractor shall not be held responsible for any existing violations of applicable building regulations or ordinances, whether cited by the appropriate authority or not. Contractor is not responsible for any abnormal or unusual preexisting conditions or any unusual or abnormal concrete footings, foundations, retaining walls, or piers required, or any unusual depth required for same, such as, but not limited to that condition caused by poor soil, lack of compaction, hillside, or other slope conditions. Correction of any such violations or abnormal conditions by Contractor shall be considered additional work and shall be dealt with as herein provided for under "Extra Work".

2. DELAYS. Contractor agrees to start and diligently pursue work through to completion, but shall not be responsible for delays for any of the following reasons: failure of the issuance of all necessary building permits within a reasonable length of time, funding of loans, disbursement of funds into funding control or escrow, acts of neglect or omission of Owner or Owner's employees or Owner's agent, acts of God, stormy or inclement weather, strikes, lockouts, boycotts, or other labor union activities, extra work ordered by Owner, acts of public enemy, riots or civil commotion, inability to secure material through regular recognized channels, imposition of Government priority or allocation of materials, failure of Owner to make payments when due, or delays caused by inspection or changes ordered by the inspectors of authorized governmental bodies, or for acts of independent contractors, or holidays, or other causes beyond Contractor's reasonable control.

3. Contractor is not responsible for matching existing paint or texture and further there is no guarantee against hairline cracks or discolorization in stucco or concrete.

OWNER'S RESPONSIBILITIES

UTILITIES

1. The Owner is responsible for water, gas, sewer and electric utilities, from the appropriate agency, to the metering device, unless otherwise agreed to in writing.

It is the Owner's responsibility, at his expense, to provide electricity and water to the site as needed by the Contractor.

ACCESS TO PROPERTY

2. Owner agrees to keep driveway clear and available for movement and parking of trucks and other equipment during normal working hours. If Owner denies access to any workmen or materialmen during the scheduled working hours, the Owner will be held in breach of this Agreement and will be liable for such breach.

FINANCING

3. The Owner is responsible for having sufficient funds to comply with this Agreement. This is a cash transaction.

INSURANCE

4. Owner will purchase insurance at his expense before any work begins. Such insurance will have course of construction, fire, vandalism, malicious mischief and other perils, clauses attached. The insurance must be in an amount at least equal to the contract price and provide that any loss is payable to the Contractor. The insurance is to cover the Owner, Contractor, Subcontractor and Construction Lender in the amount of their respective interests.

If the Owner does not purchase such insurance, the Contractor, as agent for the Owner MAY purchase it and charge such cost to the Owner.

DAMAGE OR DESTRUCTION

5. If the project or any portion of it is destroyed or damaged by fire, storm, flood, landslide, earthquake, theft or other disaster or accident, any work done by the Contractor to rebuild, etc., shall be paid for by Owner as an Extra and dealt with as herein provided for under "Extra Work".

In the event of any of the above occurrences, if the cost of replacement work, for work already done by the Contractor, exceeds twenty (20) percent of the contract price, the Owner has the option to cancel the contract but if the Owner cancels, the Contractor shall be paid for all costs incurred plus Contractor's usual fee for overhead and profit for all work performed by Contractor to date of cancellation.

OWNER'S PROPERTY

6. It is the Owner's responsibility to remove or protect any personal property including, but not limited to, carpets, drapes, furniture, driveways, lawns and shrubs, and Contractor will not be held responsible for damage to or loss of said items.

NOTICE OF COMPLETION

7. Owner agrees to sign and record a Notice of Completion within five (5) days after the project is substantially completed and ready for occupancy. Failure by the Owner to do so authorizes the Contractor to act as the Owner's agent to sign and record a Notice of Completion. This agency is irrevocable and is an agency coupled with an interest. The Contractor has the right to bar occupancy of the project by Owner or anyone else until Contractor has received all payments due under the Contract and the Notice of Completion is recorded. When the Owner or another authorized by the Owner uses and or occupies the premises then the project is conclusively completed. If a funding or joint control is used it is agreed that the control shall act as the Owner's agent and sign and record a Notice of Completion.

BOUNDARY LINES

8. The Owner represents that he owns the property where construction is to occur. It is the Owner's duty to point out boundary lines of the property and Owner is responsible for the accuracy of such lines and how they are represented on drawings. If required, the Owner will pay for a survey to affect boundary lines.

EASEMENTS, ETC.

9. Prior to construction the Owner is to give the Contractor a copy of any easements, restrictions or rights of way relating to the property. If Owner does not do so, Contractor will assume that none exist.

ENGINEERING AND GEOLOGY

10. Unless specifically agreed upon in writing between Owner and Contractor and made a part of this Agreement under "Description of Project", "Description of Materials", "Specifications" or "Plans", this agreement does not include any engineering or geology surveys, drawings, studies, reports or calculations that may be required by a public body or building authority as a condition for issuance of building permit or as a condition to securing final building inspection. The cost of any such required professional services shall be paid by Owner.

OTHER

DRAWINGS AND SPECIFICATIONS

1. The project will be constructed according to drawings and specifications that have been examined by Owner and that have been or may be signed by the parties to this contract. Unless otherwise specifically provided in the drawings or specifications, Contractor will obtain and pay for all required building permits, and Owner will pay any assessments and charges required by public bodies and utilities for financing or repaying the cost of sewers, storm drains, water service and other utilities including sewer and storm drain reimbursement charges, tax fees, revolving fund charges, hookup charges and the like.

ITEMS EXCLUDED

2. Unless specifically agreed upon in writing between Owner and Contractor and made part of this Agreement, under "Description of Work", "Description of Materials", "Specifications", or "Plans", this contract does not include:

a. Plumbing, gas, waste and water lines outside foundations of existing buildings or any required relocation or replacement of any such existing lines that may be discovered within the boundaries of any new ground floor addition.

b. Electrical service, other than addition of circuit breakers or fuse blocks to distribute electric current to new outlets;

c. Any work which may be required regarding cesspools or septic tanks;

d. Rerouting, relocating or replacing vents, pipes, ducts or conduits not shown or those encountered during construction or changes required to existing wiring, vents, pipes, ducts or conduits in areas undisturbed by construction. Unless specified elsewhere, existing wiring and electrical systems are represented by the Owner as adequate to carry load for existing structure and work to be performed herein;

e. Any additional work required for excavation or foundations due to inadequate bearing capacity or rock or any other material not removeable by ordinary hand tools;

f. Any work to correct damage caused by termites or dry rot;

g. Changes or alterations from the drawings or specifications which may be required by any public body, utility or inspector.

h. Painting, preparation, filing, finishing, grading, retaining walls, new or relocated gutters and downspouts, screen doors, weather stripping, staining, seeding, landscaping, or decorating.

Any work necessary to correct, change, alter or add the above items will be considered additional work and shall be dealt with as herein provided for under "Extra Work".

MEASUREMENTS

3. Measurements, sizes and shapes in plans and specifications are approximate and subject to field verification. Unless otherwise specified, all dimensions are exterior dimensions. In the event of a conflict between the plans, specifications, etc., and the Agreement, this Agreement is controlling. Contractor is not responsible for any existing illegal conditions.

MATERIAL REMOVED AND DEBRIS

4. Unles specifically designated by Owner in writing, prior to commencement of construction, Contractor may dispose of all material removed from structures in course of alteration. Also Contractor is to remove construction debris at end of project and leave premises in neat, broom-clean condition.

FLOOR COVERING

5. Unless specifically agreed upon in writing, floor covering is not covered under this Agreement.

ADDITIONAL REQUIREMENTS FOR COMPLETION

6. Contractor shall promptly notify Owner of any additional requirements necessary to facilitate the project's completion. Any subsequent amendment, modification or agreement which operates to alter this contract, and which is signed or initialed by Contractor and Owner, shall be deemed a part of this contract and shall be controlling in case of conflict, to the extent that it alters this contract.

EXTRA WORK

7. The Owner and Contractor must agree in writing to any modification or addition to the work covered by this contract. The Contractor shall do no extra work without the written authorization of the Owner. Any written agreement shall list the agreed price and any changes in terms, and be signed by both parties. Failure to have written authorization shall not be deemed fatal to the collection of the extra work.

For any extra work performed, Contractor shall be compensated in an amount to be determined before the extra work is performed and such amount, including Contractor's usual fee for overhead and profit shall be made as the extra work progresses, concurrently with payments, made under payments scheduled.

STANDARDS FOR SPECIFICATIONS

8. If all or any part of the following is included in this Agreement under specifications, the following will apply: All cabinets to be paint grade, or if same is noted to be other than paint grade, to be of veneer construction. All cabinet doors to be lipped construction. All inside portions such as shelves, bulkheads, and partitions may be of other species than exposed portions, but not limited to solid stock, plywood, or particle board with fixed shelves without backs. All plumbing fixtures to be white in color and selected by Contractor. All appliances and fixtures to be Builders models. Medicine cabinets to be single, recessed, and metal. Tile, if ceramic, to be domestic, non-decorator, 41/4" x 41/4". All fireplaces to be prefab with a metal flue. All extra materials remain the property of the Contractor. If any of the materials used vary from the above, such variation must be agreed upon between Contractor and Owner, in writing, and listed in this Agreement under "Specifications", "Description of Materials" or attached to this Agreement and initiated by Owner and Contractor.

CORRECTIVE WORK

9. If minor corrective or repair work remains to be finished after the project is ready for occupancy, Contractor shall perform work expeditiously and Owner shall not withhold any payment pending completion of such work.

If major corrective or repair work remains to be finished after the building is ready for occupancy, and the cost exceeds one (1) percent of the gross contract price, the Owner may withhold payment sufficient to pay for completion of the work, pending completion of the work, but may not withhold an amount which is greater.

GENERAL

10. This contract, including incorporated documents, constitutes the entire agreement of the parties. No other oral or written agreements between Contractor and Owner, regarding construction to be performed exist.

11. This agreement shall be construed in accordance with, and governed by, the laws of the State of California.

NOTICE

12. Any notice required or permitted under this contract may be given by ordinary mail sent to the address of either the Owner or Contractor as listed in this contract, but the address may be changed by written notice from one party to the other. Notice is considered received five (5) days after deposited in the mail, postage prepaid.

ARBITRATION – VALIDITY – DAMAGES

13. Any controversy or claim arising out of or related to this contract, or the breach thereof, shall be settled by arbitration in accordance with the Construction Industry Arbitration Rules of the American Arbitration Association, and judgment upon the award rendered by the Arbitrator(s) may be entered in any court having jurisdiction thereof. Disputes within the monetary limit of the Small Claims Court shall be litigated in such court at the request of either party. In case one or more of the provisions of this Agreement or any application thereof shall be invalid, unenforceable or illegal, the validity, enforceability and legality of the remaining provisions and any other application shall not in any way be impaired thereby. Any damages for which Contractor may be liable to Owner shall not, in any event, exceed the cash price of this contract.

NOTICE TO OWNER

Under the California Mechanics Lien Law any contractor, subcontractor, laborer, supplier or other person who helps to improve your property, but is not paid for his/her work or supplies, has a right to enforce a claim against your property. This means that after a court hearing, your property could be sold by a court officer and the proceeds of the sale used to satisfy the indebtedness. This can happen even if you have paid your contractor in full if the subcontractors, laborers or supplies remain unpaid.

To preserve their right to file a claim or lien against your property, certain claimants, such as subcontractors or materials suppliers, are required to provide you with a document entitled "Preliminary Notice". Original (or prime) contractors and laborers for wage do not have to provide this notice. A Primary Notice is not a lien against your property. Its purpose is to notify you of persons who may have a right to file a lien against your property if they are not paid. (Generally, the maximum time allowed for filing a claim or lien against your property is ninety (90) days after completion of your project.)

TO INSURE EXTRA PROTECTION FOR YOURSELF AND YOUR PROPERTY, YOU MAY WISH TO TAKE ONE OR MORE OF THE FOLLOWING STEPS.

1. Require that your contractor supply you with a payment and performance bond (not a license bond), which provides that the bonding company will either complete the project or pay damages up to the amount of the bond. This payment and performance bond, as well as a copy of the construction contract, should be filed with the county recorder for your further protection.

2. Require that payments be made directly to subcontractors and material suppliers through a joint control. Any joint control agreement should include the addendum approved by the Registrar of Contractors.

3. Issue joint checks for payment, made out to both your contractor and subcontractors or material suppliers involved in the project. This will help to insure that all persons due payment are actually paid.

4. After making payment on any completed phase of the project, and before making any further payments require your contractor to provide you with unconditional lien releases signed by each material supplier, subcontractor and laborer involved in that portion of the work for which payment was made. On projects involving improvements to a single family residence or a duplex owned by individuals, the persons signing these releases lose the right to file a claim against your property. In other types of construction this protection may still be important, but may not be as complete. TO PROTECT YOURSELF UNDER THIS OPTION, YOU MUST BE CERTAIN THAT ALL MATERIAL SUPPLIERS, SUBCONTRACTORS OR LABORERS HAVE SIGNED.

clause has been inserted under "Description of Project." All specifications refer to the separate specifications schedule. The start date is precise, but the completion date is "approximately within six weeks," not precise enough for the homeowner to take action if the job is completed a little late.

The small print above the Notice to the Buyer requires the homeowner to pay on time. The next paragraph suggests the option of joint control.

Please read the Notice to the Buyer. It contains sage advice. The right of recision is the three-day period in which the homeowner has the option of canceling the agreement. And read the notice on the bottom, which informs California homeowners that they have a right to demand both payment and completion bonds.

Terms and Conditions

Asbestos. If you know that asbestos is in your walls or anywhere else, it's best that you let the contractor know. On this particular job, asbestos was found in the ceiling, causing a delay in the project when asbestos-removing subs had to be brought in. *Contractor's responsibility.* I advise altering this paragraph to require permission from the owner before the contractor substitutes materials. I would also advise against allowing the warranty to be limited. Consequential damage resulting from defective materials or installation should be covered. There is also no reason why the warranty should not be transferrable or why it must necessarily be limited to one year.

Items Not Responsibility of Contractor

Delays. Delete the clause that forgives changes caused by inspector-ordered delays. It should be the contractor's responsibility to do the job right in the first place. And acts of subcontractors are absolutely the responsibility of the contractor. Out goes that clause as well.

The "paint matching and cracks" paragraph is an item that you should negotiate with the contractor and modify to suit the realities of the particular project.

Owner's Responsibilities

Utilities. This simply states that the utilities suppliers are responsible for bringing the utilities as far as the meter, that it is not the contractor's job, and that any utilities that the contractor needs in order to perform his or her work shall be provided by the homeowners at their own expense.

Insurance. It is advisable that you carry sufficient insurance to protect your property *at all times*, even if no contractor is involved.

Owner's Property

Negotiate the specifics of this paragraph to suit your needs and specify the new agreement in writing. Delete and initial this paragraph unless you decide to let it stand.

Notice of Completion

The fourth and fifth sentences should be deleted because you may not want to make final payment until all liens have been cleared, which means that you will want to wait for the lien notification time to lapse.

Items Excluded

If any work being contracted for is listed under the heading "Items Excluded," make sure that such work is spelled out clearly in the specifications and cross that category of work out of this paragraph and initial it along with the contractor.

Measurements

If measurements need to be precise, eliminate this sentence and replace it with one saying that all shapes, specifications, and measurements are precise.

Standards for Specifications

This entire paragraph is unnecessary and should be deleted and initialed because you should list all of the specifications clearly in your contract. Don't allow this paragraph to prevail out of default because you have failed to specify in the contract what kind of materials you expect.

Corrective Work

Eliminate the part of the sentence that reads, "Owner shall not withhold any payment pending completion of such work." It makes no sense to pay for the uncompleted parts of the project.

Notice to Owner

We've been all through this. I would not put much faith in suggestion #3. The contractor will have to get his share of the payments paid exclusively to himself and could fudge on the proportions that go to subs and that go to him.

Remember: Each preprinted contract may vary, and I have given you this one only as a sample of how to work with and understand contracts.

Date: February 19, 1991
Owners:
Project:
Revised: February 21, 1991
               Revisions in bold.

PAYMENT SCHEDULE

$ 1,450	Down Payment
5,000	Day Job Starts
5,001	Upon Start of Skylights
5,002	Upon Start of Drywall
1,500	**Upon Start of Acoustic**
1,422	**Upon Completion**
19,375	**Total Sale Price**

× _____   × _____

[homeowner]   By [contractor]

Date _____

The Payment Schedule

The down payment is $1,450. California law limits down payments to a maximum of $1,000 or 10 percent of the total job price, whichever is less. However, the contractor is allowed to charge for any work that has already been done on behalf of the client. In this case the contractor has done substantial planning in determining his bid, so it was fair for him to include those costs in the down payment.

The $5,000 first payment is more than 25 percent of the cost of the total job. Personally, I would be reluctant to pay that much up front to a contractor whom I didn't know. I would have negotiated for a lower initial payment and either larger subsequent payments or additional payments during the course of the job.

There are no dates on the schedule, which is fine because the contract contains start and completion dates. If the various parts of the job are running late, it means that the contractor gets paid late. However, this type of schedule is deficient in that a dishonest contractor could start the skylights and demand payment, then start the drywall one week later and the acoustic four days after that. He could thereby collect almost all the money early in the job. And then images of warm Virgin Islands beaches could start looming in his head. And we don't want him taking a premature—and permanent—vacation.

This would be a more desirable version of the same schedule:

$ 1,450	Down Payment
2,000	Day Job Starts
5,001	Upon Start of Skylights but no sooner than 10 days after start of job
5,002	Upon Start of Drywall but no sooner than 20 days after start of job
3,000	Upon Start of Acoustic but no sooner than 30 days after start of job
1,500	Upon completion
1,422	30 Days After Completion
$19,375	Total Sale Price

This schedule gives the homeowner time to ascertain that the suppliers and subs have been paid. It also prevents the contractor from receiving most of his payments early in the job and reserves final payment until after sufficient time for those who might claim mechanics' liens to notify the homeowner. (Check such time limitations for your state.)

Appendix C
Sample Specifications Schedule

Date: February 18, 1991
Revised: February 21, 1991
            Revisions in Bold

Owners:
Project:

Specifications

Schedule #1

Re: Various Remodeling Work Including
            Three Skylights and Expanding
            Playroom.

Note: Work performed may not necessarily be
            executed in same order as written.

PULL-DOWN STAIRS   Supply and Install

1. Cut opening for pull-down stairs (see plan).
2. Move electrical as necessary.
3. Rework drywall as necessary and make ready for
    painting.
4. **Install four sheets of plywood around pull-down
    stairs. Plywood will be cut around obstructions.**
    $(32f^2 \times 4)$

SKYLIGHT OVER STAIRWAY   Supply and Install

1. 2' × 4' double-dome skylight, tinted. Bristolite or equal in quality.
2. Frame well like a trapezoid. Skylight will fit between two existing rafters.
3. Rework roof shake shingles to make weatherproof and consistent. If new shingles are used it will be an obvious color difference.
4. Drywall well and make ready for painting.
5. Provide outlet for track light, **install in well** and use existing circuit on second floor. Owners supply light fixture. 3 foot fixture (4 feet will fit but be big)
6. **Remove light on ceiling at skylight over stairs.**

LIVING ROOM, SKYLIGHTS AND FOYER WINDOW   Supply and Install

1. Two 2' × 4' Bristolite double-dome tinted skylights installed in between roof rafters of living room (see drawings).
2. Fixed window **2'6" × 5' bronze anodized aluminum tempered glass** for foyer, match existing type windows and detail on exterior as close as possible.
3. Finish drywall to make ready for painting by others.
4. Repair holes in ceiling at stairway, **and over dining room light.**
5. Rework roof shingles to make weatherproof and consistent. If new shingles are used it will be an obvious color difference.

FIREPLACE

DELETED

MOVE WALL TOWARD DECK   Supply and Install

1. Add new wall 3' into existing deck. Save one half of existing closet and reuse door.

2. Remove existing wall at deck (see plan).

3. Rework stucco and drywall to match existing as close as possible.

4. Change existing window to smaller size: 2'6" × 3'6", **bronze anodized window and tempered glass.**

5. 8'0" × 6'8" wood sliding door with screen in **10 light** glass cut-up style by Cal Classic. Slides to right from outside.

6. Level off playroom floor with plywood.

7. **Save tile shelf if possible.**

8. **Relocate exterior light and plug** and phone jack.

OTHER ELECTRICAL Supply and Install

1. Plug and simple light in attic.

2. Simple overhead light in **storage area.**

3. **DELETED**

4. **Cable television by owners.**

5. **Add plug in playroom.**

ACOUSTIC CEILING Supply and Install

1. Respray over existing ceiling on first floor.

2. Same for second floor hall ceiling (not bedrooms).

3. **No acoustic spray on wells of three skylights.**

NOTES (Also see contract.)

1. Working drawings, engineering, school tax and necessary permits provided by Contractor.

2. Contractor will provide toilet facilities for construction workers.

3. Contractor will pay owners for any unusually high phone bill for interoffice communications during construction. Owners should notify Contractor for reimbursement.

4. Construction site will be left in orderly fashion during construction. A debris pile location will be agreed upon by owners and Contractor prior to much build-

up. Debris will be hauled away after a truckload is accumulated.

5. Owners allow Contractor to install a job sign at an obvious location during construction period.

6. Contractor will make secure any openings from construction for optimum security of owners' property. Owners will lend key to Contractor, and the key will be left secure in lockbox attached to the doorknob.

7. Contractor is a state-licensed general building contractor with workers' compensation and general liability insurances.

8. Contractor will secure owners' property being worked on against inclement weather during the construction period.

9. Contractor will protect carpets and floors walked on constantly by construction workers. Owners are responsible for cleanup of dust that settles from construction work.

10. Work hours are from 7 A.M. to 5:30 P.M., Monday through Friday, unless otherwise agreed.

11. Water and electricity will be provided by owner.

12. Extra work, inclement weather, and delays caused by inspectors will extend expected completion date.

13. Soil analysis is not included unless otherwise mentioned. This is not usually required.

14. Supplied and installed by owners (others): floor covering, carpets, painting, security systems (unless otherwise indicated above), and anything specifically not mentioned. Specifications supersede drawings.

15. Supplied by owners and installed by Contractor: any kitchen appliances, bathroom accessories such as toilet paper holder, towel bar, furniture mirrors, medicine cabinets, etc.; surface-mounted light fixtures; decorative hardware.

16. Contractor's scope of work shall not include the identification, detection, abatement, encapsulation, or removal of asbestos or similar hazardous substances. In the event that Contractor encounters any such products or materials in the course of performing its work, Contractor shall have the right to discontinue

its work and remove its employees from the project until no such products or materials, or any hazard, exist, as the case may require, and Contractor shall receive an extension of time to complete its work hereunder and compensation for delays encountered as a result of such situation and correction.

17. If there are any leftover building supplies from work done, then these materials are the property of Contractor.

18. Owners agree not to contract with any employee or subcontractor used by Contractor during or after construction unless agreed to by Contractor.

19. All work shall be performed per local building codes. If additional work is required by the building department other than indicated above, then that will be an extra cost to the owner.

20. Upon end of project Contractor and owners will meet and agree upon incidental items left to be completed. A Completion Punch List will be drawn up in writing and signed. Contractor will expeditiously complete such items that constitute completion of job. Upon agreement of punch list owners agree to sign Notice of Completion, if one exists, and agree not to hold back monies due over the amount of the work left to complete.

21. Extra work, if any, will be paid in advance by owners.

22. Color renderings and decorator boards are an approximation of the final result. Blueprint drawings and written specifications supersede renderings and decorator boards.

23. Any advance payments are used for holding and purchasing special-order items and payment for services rendered. Designer, engineering, and architectual fees are included in sale price and represent 10 percent of sale price.

24. Allowance items are the estimated cost to purchase necessary material at contractor's cost plus tax and delivery. Allowances are used when exact materials haven't been selected, just approximated.

25. Testimonial letters given to Contractor can be used in Introductory Packs for prospective clients to read, unless otherwise mentioned.

Specifications

As far as protecting the homeowner goes, this schedule is deficient. I will point out some deficiencies in each schedule section, and I challenge you to rewrite the other possible deficiencies. This is a good exercise, so don't shunt it aside. I know you, and you need the practice.

Pull-Down Stairs. The brand name and model and the dimensions are not included. Neither is a description of what the finished installation will look like. What's wrong with item 4?

Skylight Over Stairway. It does not specify *where* over the stairway. What's missing from items 4, 5, and 6?

Living Room, Skylights, and Foyer Window. *Where* the window goes is not specified. Does it replace an existing window? What is missing from item 3?

Move Wall Toward Deck. Item 1 is very deficient—it gives the contractor too much leeway. There should be more of an explanation of what is required. What happens where the other half of the closet is to be eliminated? Reuse the *deck* door or the *closet* door? What will the new wall be made of? What about interior wall electrical outlets?

Other Electrical. What does "plug" mean? Where does it go? What is a "simple" light? And where does it go? What's wrong with numbers 2 and 5?

Acoustic Ceiling. There is no description of what is meant by "acoustic ceiling."

Notes. This is the sign of a professional contractor. It deals with such odds and ends as engineering, permits, toilet facilities, phone bills, neatness, security, credentials, work hours (too early for neighbors), utilities, items to be supplied by owners and by contractor, asbestos—which was later found in the ceiling and required changes in the project—and a fair method for dealing with job completion (item 20).

Appendix D

Sample Change Order

Date: April 19, 1991

Owners:
Project:

Schedule 2

$3,444.00	Add electrical recess lighting per plans.
250.00	Correct electrical
3,694.00	**Total Upgrade**

X _____

By [contractor]

X _____

[homeowner]

Date _____

On this job the one change order that was written up was labeled "Schedule 2." It contains the date of the change order, a description of the additional work to be done, the cost of the work and . . . nothing else. It does not include a description of the fixtures to be installed. Nor does it include information as to where in the schedule the additional work will be done and whether or not it will extend the completion date.

"Correct Electrical" gives the contractor carte blanche to do as he pleases. What does it mean?

As I stated earlier, the contractor on this job was of the highest honesty and integrity, so the couple involved had no serious problems and were very happy with the job. However, if you are not more diligent than they, you could find yourself contracting for trouble. Be careful and be explicit. Please.

Glossary

Amortized loan. A loan paid back in installments. The installments reduce the amount of the principal of the loan and fully pay it off within a given period of time. In the event that variables enter into the paying off of the debt and the (monthly) payments no longer cover the full principal installments, the loan is no longer *fully* amortized, which results in an increase in the number of payments required to pay off the principal.

Arbitration. The settlement of a dispute by the reliance upon a mutually agreed-upon party to hear both sides and to impartially reach a solution. Arbitration may be binding or nonbinding. In the case of contractor-related disputes, the arbitration usually binds both parties to accept the findings of the arbitrator.

Balloon payment. A payment due at the end of a fixed period of time that pays off the entire principal balance of a debt. It is usually preceded by a series of installment payments that pay off the accruing interest on the debt.

Bond. An insurance agreement by which the insurer guarantees payment to compensate a third party for losses incurred as a result of some contingency (or possible occurrence) or a failure to perform on the part of the insured. In contractor agreements a bond is provided to guarantee to the homeowner that in the event the contractor fails to meet the contract requirements, the bond issuer will pay for losses incurred by the homeowner. The amount that the homeowner may collect may be limited by the terms and the financial limit of the bond.

Change order. A written agreement that is an amendment to a remodeling or repair contract. It includes information such as, but not limited to, changes in materials, prices, dates of performance, work to be done, additions, and deletions. It should be as completely spelled out as the original contract and should be signed and dated by both parties.

Collateral. Something of value used to secure a loan. The collateral is held as security until the loan is paid off.

Completion bond. A bond (see above) which guarantees that if a contract is not fulfilled, the issuer of the bond will pay any additional funds needed to complete the job as contracted for.

Contractor. As used in this book, a person or company that agrees to improve, repair, remodel, or build a residence or a part thereof in exchange for an agreed-upon payment.

Equity. The value of a property above the total amount of debts owed on it. These debts may include mortgages, liens, and home equity loans.

Final completion. The total and absolute finishing of a contracted job— the state of the job in which no work is left to be done, and therefore final payment is appropriate.

General contractor. A contractor who is hired to do a job involving several different specialties that must be coordinated (as opposed to a specialty contractor).

Interest rate. The percentage of a loan principal that is charged annually by the lender. The figure is usually expressed as an annual charge, and payments are commonly made on a monthly basis—the annual interest rate being divided by twelve.

Liability insurance. An insurance policy carried in order to protect a homeowner from lawsuits for injuries or losses suffered by others on the homeowner's property. It is advisable that the contractor be required to carry such insurance in order to protect the homeowner from claims brought by the contractor's workers or from others on the property who might be injured as a result of actions by the contractor's workers.

License. A certificate issued by the state or local government that allows a contractor to do business in that jurisdiction. Licensing may require the contractor to pass examinations, present proof of competence, pay licensing fees, or show proof of insurance or proof of surety bonding.

Lien. A claim upon property for payment of some debt, obligation, or duty. Usually, unless such liens are paid off, the property in question cannot be sold. In some instances, the lien holder can force the sale of the property in order to pay off the debt. (See *Mechanic's lien.*)

Lien waiver. A written statement that relieves a homeowner of any obligations to pay off debts. A waiver is usually issued by a contractor, subcontractor, or materials supplier to assure the homeowner that no debts are due. This is usually done to make it safe for the homeowner to make scheduled payments.

Mechanic's lien. A lien (see above) imposed upon a property for the purpose of securing priority of payment for the value of work performed and materials furnished in building or repairing a property. Usually claimed by material suppliers or contractors.

Mediation. A voluntary process by which a preselected individual attempts to bring about an agreement or reconciliation between two contending parties. Usually attempted before the contending parties seek more stringent solutions in law, such as arbitration or lawsuit.

Points. The charge levied by a lender for a loan, above and in addition to the interest charges. The term *points* refers to percentage points charged. Example: A $100,000 loan with an annual interest rate of 9 percent and a loan fee of 1.5 points means, in simplified terms, that the borrower will pay 9 percent interest on the balance of the loan each year and will also have to pay $1,500 up front to the bank for the loan itself.

Specialty contractor. A repair or building contractor who works in one area of specialization. Examples are electricians, painters, plumbers, plasterers, air-conditioning installers and repairers, masons, drywall installers, and carpenters.

Subcontractor. A contractor who is hired by a general contractor or by another specialty contractor to perform some aspect of a contracting job.

Substantial performance or substantial completion. A point in the contracting project whereby the work is finished except for minor variances or incomplete aspects of the job. Under law, substantial performance is usually enough for the homeowner to be required to pay for the contracted job, minus the value of the work that has not yet been completed.

Supplier. A party who provides materials for a home improvement or repair project.

Waiver. See *Lien waiver*.

Workmen's compensation insurance. A policy issued by an insurance company that provides for injury, suffering, and income compensation for employees. In home improvement, repair, or building projects, if the contractor does not provide such protection, the homeowner may be sued by an injured employee. It is therefore advisable that homeowners insist upon such coverage and confirm the coverage with the contractor's insurer.

Bibliography

American Arbitration Association. *Construction Contract Disputes: How They May Be Resolved*. New York: May 1990.

California Board of Architectural Examiners. *Consumer's Guide to Hiring an Architect*. Sacramento: State of California Department of Consumer Affairs, October 1988.

Chouke, Johnny. *Home Repair Scams . . . How to Avoid Them*. New York: Boardroom Books, November 15, 1990.

Council of Better Business Bureaus. *Annual Inquiry and Complaint Summary—1990*. Arlington, Va.: 1991.

Council of Better Business Bureaus. *Tips on . . . Home Improvements*. Arlington, Va.: 1978; revised 1988.

Frechette, Leon A. *The Helping Hands Guide to Hiring a Remodeling Contractor*. Spokane, Wash.: C.R.S., Inc., 1988.

Garr, Doug. "Choosing a Contractor." *Reader's Digest*, September 1989.

Hallman, Guy. "Don't Get Soaked." *The Miami Herald*, May 20, 1990.

Hashagen, Werner R. *How to Get It Built Better–Faster–For Less*. La Jolla, Calif.: Werner R. Hashagen & Associates, 1985.

Home Owners Warranty Corporation. *The HOW-to Guide to Remodeling*. Arlington, Va.: 1991.

Milko, George, Kay Ostberg, and Theresa Mehan Rudy in association with HALT. *Everyday Contracts, Protecting Your Rights: A Step-by-Step Guide*. New York: Random House, 1991.

National Association of Home Builders—Remodelors Council. *How to Choose a Remodeler Who's on the Level*. Washington, D.C.: 1991.

———. *1991 Analysis of State Contractor Licensing Laws*. Washington, D.C.: 1991.

National Association of the Remodeling Industry. *NARI 1991 Summary of Contractor Licensing Laws*. Arlington, Va.: 1991.

Philbin, Tom. "10 Common Home Repair Scams . . . and How to Avoid Them. *Woman's Day,* March 20, 1990.

State Bar of California. *What Should I Know Before I Sign?* San Francisco: 1980.

Index